# Wonderful Adventures of
# Mrs. Seacole in Many Lands

THE SCHOMBURG LIBRARY OF
NINETEENTH-CENTURY BLACK WOMEN WRITERS

*General Editor*, Henry Louis Gates, Jr.

Titles are listed chronologically; collections that include works published over a
span of years are listed according to the publication date of their initial work.

# Wonderful Adventures of Mrs. Seacole in Many Lands

MARY SEACOLE

*With an Introduction by*
WILLIAM L. ANDREWS

෬ ෬ ෬

෬ ෬ ෬

OXFORD UNIVERSITY PRESS
*New York    Oxford*

Oxford University Press

Oxford   New York   Toronto
Delhi   Bombay   Calcutta   Madras   Karachi
Petaling Jaya   Singapore   Hong Kong   Tokyo
Nairobi   Dar es Salaam   Cape Town
Melbourne   Auckland

and associated companies in
Berlin   Ibadan

Copyright © 1988 by Oxford University Press, Inc.

First published in 1988 by Oxford University Press, Inc.,
198 Madison Avenue, New York, New York 10016-4314

First issued as an Oxford University Press paperback, 1990

Oxford is a registered trademark of Oxford University Press

Library of Congress Cataloging-in-Publication Data

Seacole, Mary, 1805–1881.
Wonderful adventures of Mrs. Seacole in many lands/with an
introduction by William L. Andrews.
p.   cm.—(The Schomburg library of nineteenth-century black
women writers)
Reprint. Originally published: London: J. Blackwood, 1857.
1. Crimean War, 1853–1856—Personal narratives, Jamaican.
2. Seacole, Mary, 1805–1881.   3. Blacks—Jamaica—Biography.
I. Title.   II. Series.
DK215.S43   1988      947'.073—dc19      87-25375
ISBN 0-19-505249-8
ISBN 0-19-505267-6 (set)
ISBN 0-19-506672-3 (PBK.)

6 8 10 9 7 5

Printed in the United States of America

The
Schomburg Library
of
Nineteenth-Century
Black Women Writers
is
Dedicated
in Memory
of
PAULINE AUGUSTA COLEMAN GATES

*1916–1987*

# PUBLISHER'S NOTE

# FOREWORD
## *In Her Own Write*

*Henry Louis Gates, Jr.*

One muffled strain in the Silent South, a jarring chord and a vague and uncomprehended cadenza has been and still is the Negro. And of that muffled chord, the one mute and voiceless note has been the sadly expectant Black Woman, . . . .

The "other side" has not been represented by one who "lives there." And not many can more sensibly realize and more accurately tell the weight and the fret of the "long dull pain" than the open-eyed but hitherto voiceless Black Woman of America.

. . . as our Caucasian barristers are not to blame if they cannot *quite* put themselves in the dark man's place, neither should the dark man be wholly expected fully and adequately to reproduce the exact Voice of the Black Woman.

—ANNA JULIA COOPER, *A Voice From the South* (1892)

The birth of the Afro-American literary tradition occurred in 1773, when Phillis Wheatley published a book of poetry. Despite the fact that her book garnered for her a remarkable amount of attention, Wheatley's journey to the printer had been a most arduous one. Sometime in 1772, a young African girl walked demurely into a room in Boston to undergo an oral examination, the results of which would determine the direction of her life and work. Perhaps she was shocked upon entering the appointed room. For there, perhaps gath-

vii

ered in a semicircle, sat eighteen of Boston's most notable citizens. Among them were John Erving, a prominent Boston merchant; the Reverend Charles Chauncy, pastor of the Tenth Congregational Church; and John Hancock, who would later gain fame for his signature on the Declaration of Independence. At the center of this group was His Excellency, Thomas Hutchinson, governor of Massachusetts, with Andrew Oliver, his lieutenant governor, close by his side.

Why had this august group been assembled? Why had it seen fit to summon this young African girl, scarcely eighteen years old, before it? This group of "the most respectable Characters in *Boston*," as it would later define itself, had assembled to question closely the African adolescent on the slender sheaf of poems that she claimed to have "written by herself." We can only speculate on the nature of the questions posed to the fledgling poet. Perhaps they asked her to identify and explain—for all to hear—exactly who were the Greek and Latin gods and poets alluded to so frequently in her work. Perhaps they asked her to conjugate a verb in Latin or even to translate randomly selected passages from the Latin, which she and her master, John Wheatley, claimed that she "had made some Progress in." Or perhaps they asked her to recite from memory key passages from the texts of John Milton and Alexander Pope, the two poets by whom the African claimed to be most directly influenced. We do not know.

We do know, however, that the African poet's responses were more than sufficient to prompt the eighteen august gentlemen to compose, sign, and publish a two-paragraph "Attestation," an open letter "To the Publick" that prefaces Phillis Wheatley's book and that reads in part:

We whose Names are under-written, do assure the World, that the Poems specified in the following Page, were (as we verily believe) written by Phillis, a young Negro Girl, who was but a few Years since, brought an uncultivated Barbarian from *Africa*, and has ever since been, and now is, under the Disadvantage of serving as a Slave in a Family in this Town. She has been examined by some of the best Judges, and is thought qualified to write them.

So important was this document in securing a publisher for Wheatley's poems that it forms the signal element in the prefatory matter preceding her *Poems on Various Subjects, Religious and Moral,* published in London in 1773.

Without the published "Attestation," Wheatley's publisher claimed, few would believe that an African could possibly have written poetry all by herself. As the eighteen put the matter clearly in their letter, "Numbers would be ready to suspect they were not really the Writings of Phillis." Wheatley and her master, John Wheatley, had attempted to publish a similar volume in 1772 in Boston, but Boston publishers had been incredulous. One year later, "Attestation" in hand, Phillis Wheatley and her master's son, Nathaniel Wheatley, sailed for England, where they completed arrangements for the publication of a volume of her poems with the aid of the Countess of Huntington and the Earl of Dartmouth.

This curious anecdote, surely one of the oddest oral examinations on record, is only a tiny part of a larger, and even more curious, episode in the Enlightenment. Since the beginning of the sixteenth century, Europeans had wondered aloud whether or not the African "species of men," as they were most commonly called, *could* ever create formal literature, could ever master "the arts and sciences." If they could, the argument ran, then the African variety of humanity was fundamentally related to the European variety. If not, then it seemed clear that the African was destined by nature to be a slave. This was the burden shouldered by Phillis Wheatley when she successfully defended herself and the authorship of her book against counterclaims and doubts.

Indeed, with her successful defense, Wheatley launched two traditions at once—the black American literary tradition *and* the black woman's literary tradition. If it is extraordinary that not just one but both of these traditions were founded simultaneously by a black woman—certainly an event unique in the history of literature—it is also ironic that this important fact of common, coterminous literary origins seems to have escaped most scholars.

That the progenitor of the black literary tradition was a woman means, in the most strictly literal sense, that all subsequent black writers have evolved in a matrilinear line of descent, and that each, consciously or unconsciously, has extended and revised a canon whose foundation was the poetry of a black woman. Early black writers seem to have been keenly aware of Wheatley's founding role, even if most of her white reviewers were more concerned with the implications of her race than her gender. Jupiter Hammon, for example, whose 1760 broadside "An Evening Thought. Salvation by Christ, With Penitential Cries" was the first individual poem published by a black American, acknowledged Wheatley's influence by selecting her as the subject of his second broadside, "An Address to Miss Phillis Wheatly [*sic*], Ethiopian Poetess, in Boston," which was published at Hartford in 1778. And George Moses Horton, the second Afro-American to publish a book of poetry in English (1829), brought out in 1838 an edition of his *Poems By A Slave* bound together with Wheatley's work. Indeed, for fifty-six years, between 1773 and 1829, when Horton published *The Hope of Liberty*, Wheatley was the *only* black person to have published a book of imaginative literature in English. So central was this black woman's role in the shaping of the Afro-American literary tradition that, as one historian has maintained, the history of the reception of Phillis Wheatley's poetry *is* the history of Afro-American literary criticism. Well into the nineteenth century, Wheatley and the black literary tradition were the same entity.

But Wheatley is not the only black woman writer who stands as a pioneering figure in Afro-American literature. Just as Wheatley gave birth to the genre of black poetry, Ann Plato was the first Afro-American to publish a book of essays (1841) and Harriet E. Wilson was the first black person to publish a novel in the United States (1859).

Despite this pioneering role of black women in the tradition, however, many of their contributions before this century have been all but lost or unrecognized. As Hortense Spillers observed as recently as 1983,

> With the exception of a handful of autobiographical narratives from the nineteenth century, the black woman's realities are virtually suppressed until the period of the Harlem Renaissance and later. Essentially the black woman as artist, as intellectual spokesperson for her own cultural apprenticeship, has not existed before, for anyone. At the source of [their] own symbol-making task, [the community of black women writers] confronts, therefore, a tradition of work that is quite recent, its continuities, broken and sporadic.

Until now, it has been extraordinarily difficult to establish the formal connections between early black women's writing and that of the present, precisely because our knowledge of their work has been broken and sporadic. Phillis Wheatley, for example, while certainly the most reprinted and discussed poet in the tradition, is also one of the least understood. Ann Plato's seminal work, *Essays* (which includes biographies and poems), has not been reprinted since it was published a cen-

tury and a half ago. And Harriet Wilson's *Our Nig,* her
compelling novel of a black woman's expanding consciousness in a racist Northern antebellum environment, never received even *one* review or comment at a time when virtually
*all* works written by black people were heralded by abolition-
ists as salient arguments against the existence of human slavery. Many of the books reprinted in this set experienced a
similar fate, the most dreadful fate for an author: that of
being ignored then relegated to the obscurity of the rare book
section of a university library. We can only wonder how
many other texts in the black woman's tradition have been
lost to this generation of readers or remain unclassified or
uncatalogued and, hence, unread.

    This was not always so, however. Black women writers
dominated the final decade of the nineteenth century, perhaps
spurred to publish by an 1886 essay entitled "The Coming
American Novelist," which was published in *Lippincott's
Monthly Magazine* and written by "A Lady From Philadel-
phia." This pseudonymous essay argued that the "Great
American Novel" would be written by a black person. Her
argument is so curious that it deserves to be repeated:

> When we come to formulate our demands of the Coming
> American Novelist, we will agree that he must be native-
> born. His ancestors may come from where they will, but we
> must give him a birthplace and have the raising of him. Still,
> the longer his family has been here the better he will represent
> us. Suppose he should have no country but ours, no traditions
> but those he has learned here, no longings apart from us, no
> future except in our future—the orphan of the world, he
> finds with us his home. And with all this, suppose he refuses
> to be fused into that grand conglomerate we call the "Amer-
> ican type." With us, he is not of us. He is original, he has
> humor, he is tender, he is passive and fiery, he has been

taught what we call justice, and he has his own opinion about
it. He has suffered everything a poet, a dramatist, a novelist
need suffer before he comes to have his lips anointed. And
with it all he is in one sense a spectator, a little out of the
race. How would these conditions go towards forming an
original development? In a word, suppose the coming novelist
is of African origin? When one comes to consider the subject,
there is no improbability in it. One thing is certain,—our
great novel will not be written by the typical American.

An atypical American, indeed. Not only would the great
American novel be written by an African-American, it would
be written by an African-American *woman:*

Yet farther: I have used the generic masculine pronoun
because it is convenient; but Fate keeps revenge in store. It
was a woman who, taking the wrongs of the African as her
theme, wrote the novel that awakened the world to their
reality, and why should not the coming novelist be a woman
as well as an African? She—the woman of that race—has
some claims on Fate which are not yet paid up.

It is these claims on fate that we seek to pay by publishing
The Schomburg Library of Nineteenth-Century Black Women
Writers.

This theme would be repeated by several black women
authors, most notably by Anna Julia Cooper, a prototypical
black feminist whose 1892 *A Voice From the South* can be
considered to be one of the original texts of the black feminist movement. It was Cooper who first analyzed the fal-
lacy of referring to "the Black man" when speaking of black
people and who argued that just as white men cannot speak
through the consciousness of black men, neither can black
*men* "fully and adequately . . . reproduce the exact Voice of
the Black Woman." Gender and race, she argues, cannot be

conflated, except in the instance of a black woman's voice, and it is this voice which must be uttered and to which we must listen. As Cooper puts the matter so compellingly:

> It is not the intelligent woman vs. the ignorant woman; nor the white woman vs. the black, the brown, and the red,—it is not even the cause of woman vs. man. Nay, 'tis woman's strongest vindication for speaking that *the world needs to hear her voice*. It would be subversive of every human interest that the cry of one-half the human family be stifled. Woman in stepping from the pedestal of statue-like inactivity in the domestic shrine, and daring to think and move and speak,— to undertake to help shape, mold, and direct the thought of her age, is merely completing the circle of the world's vision. Hers is every interest that has lacked an interpreter and a defender. Her cause is linked with that of every agony that has been dumb—every wrong that needs a voice.
>
> It is no fault of man's that he has not been able to see truth from her standpoint. It does credit both to his head and heart that no greater mistakes have been committed or even wrongs perpetrated while she sat making tatting and snipping paper flowers. Man's own innate chivalry and the mutual interdependence of their interests have insured his treating her cause, in the main at least, as his own. And he is pardonably surprised and even a little chagrined, perhaps, to find his legislation not considered "perfectly lovely" in every respect. But in any case his work is only impoverished by her remaining dumb. The world has had to limp along with the wobbling gait and one-sided hesitancy of a man with one eye. Suddenly the bandage is removed from the other eye and the whole body is filled with light. It sees a circle where before it saw a segment. The darkened eye restored, every member rejoices with it.

The myopic sight of the darkened eye can only be restored when the full range of the black woman's voice, with its own special timbres and shadings, remains mute no longer.

Similarly, Victoria Earle Matthews, an author of short stories and essays, and a cofounder in 1896 of the National Association of Colored Women, wrote in her stunning essay, "The Value of Race Literature" (1895), that "when the literature of our race is developed, it will of necessity be different in all essential points of greatness, true heroism and real Christianity from what we may at the present time, for convenience, call American literature." Matthews argued that this great tradition of Afro-American literature would be the textual outlet "for the unnaturally suppressed inner lives which our people have been compelled to lead." Once these "unnaturally suppressed inner lives" of black people are unveiled, no "grander diffusion of mental light" will shine more brightly, she concludes, than that of the articulate Afro-American woman:

> And now comes the question, What part shall we women play in the Race Literature of the future? . . . within the compass of one small journal ["Woman's Era"] we have struck out a new line of departure—a journal, a record of Race interests gathered from all parts of the United States, carefully selected, moistened, winnowed and garnered by the ablest intellects of educated colored women, shrinking at no lofty theme, shirking no serious duty, aiming at every possible excellence, and determined to do their part in the future uplifting of the race.
>
> If twenty women, by their concentrated efforts in one literary movement, can meet with such success as has engendered, planned out, and so successfully consummated this convention, what much more glorious results, what wider spread success, what grander diffusion of mental light will not come forth at the bidding of the enlarged hosts of women writers, already called into being by the stimulus of your efforts?
>
> And here let me speak one word for my journalistic sisters

who have already entered the broad arena of journalism. Before the "Woman's Era" had come into existence, no one except themselves can appreciate the bitter experience and sore disappointments under which they have at all times been compelled to pursue their chosen vocations.

If their brothers of the press have had their difficulties to contend with, I am here as a sister journalist to state, from the fullness of knowledge, that their task has been an easy one compared with that of the colored woman in journalism.

Woman's part in Race Literature, as in Race building, is the most important part and has been so in all ages. . . . All through the most remote epochs she has done her share in literature. . . .

One of the most important aspects of this set is the republication of the salient texts from 1890 to 1910, which literary historians could well call "The Black Woman's Era." In addition to Mary Helen Washington's definitive edition of Cooper's *A Voice From the South*, we have reprinted two novels by Amelia Johnson, Frances Harper's *Iola Leroy*, two novels by Emma Dunham Kelley, Alice Dunbar-Nelson's two impressive collections of short stories, and Pauline Hopkins's three serialized novels as well as her monumental novel, *Contending Forces*—all published between 1890 and 1910. Indeed, black women published more works of fiction in these two decades than black men had published in the previous half century. Nevertheless, this great achievement has been ignored.

Moreover, the writings of nineteenth-century Afro-American women in general have remained buried in obscurity, accessible only in research libraries or in overpriced and poorly edited reprints. Many of these books have never been reprinted at all; in some instances only one or two copies are extant. In these works of fiction, poetry, autobiography, biography, essays, and journalism resides the mind of the nineteenth-century Afro-American woman. Until these works are made readily available to teachers and their students, a significant segment of the black tradition will remain silent.

Oxford University Press, in collaboration with the Schomburg Center for Research in Black Culture, is publishing thirty volumes of these compelling works, each of which contains an introduction by an expert in the field. The set includes such rare texts as Johnson's *The Hazeley Family* and *Clarence and Corinne*, Plato's *Essays*, the most complete edition of Phillis Wheatley's poems and letters, Emma Dunham Kelley's pioneering novel *Megda*, several previously unpublished stories and a novel by Alice Dunbar-Nelson, and the first collected volumes of Pauline Hopkins's three serialized novels and Frances Harper's poetry. We also present four volumes of poetry by such women as Mary Eliza Tucker Lambert, Adah Menken, Josephine Heard, and Maggie Johnson. Numerous slave and spiritual narratives, a newly discovered novel—*Four Girls at Cottage City*—by Emma Dunham Kelley (-Hawkins), and the first American edition of *Wonderful Adventures of Mrs. Seacole in Many Lands* are also among the texts included.

In addition to resurrecting the works of black women authors, it is our hope that this set will facilitate the resurrection of the Afro-American woman's literary tradition itself by unearthing its nineteenth-century roots. In the works of Nella Larsen and Jessie Fauset, Zora Neale Hurston and Ann Petry, Lorraine Hansberry and Gwendolyn Brooks, Paule Marshall and Toni Cade Bambara, Audre Lorde and Rita Dove, Toni Morrison and Alice Walker, Gloria Naylor and Jamaica Kincaid, these roots have branched luxuriantly. The eighteenth- and nineteenth-century authors whose works are presented in this set founded and nurtured the black women's literary tradition, which must be revived, explicated, analyzed, and debated before we can understand more completely the formal shaping of this tradition within a tradition, a coded literary universe through which, regrettably, we are only just beginning to navigate our way. As Anna Cooper said nearly one hundred years ago, we have been blinded by the loss of sight in one eye and have therefore been unable to detect the full *shape* of the Afro-American literary tradition.

Literary works configure into a tradition not because of some mystical collective unconscious determined by the biology of race or gender, but because writers read other writers and *ground* their representations of experience in models of language provided largely by other writers to whom they feel akin. It is through this mode of literary revision, amply evident in the *texts* themselves—in formal echoes, recast metaphors, even in parody—that a "tradition" emerges and defines itself.

This is formal bonding, and it is only through formal bonding that we can know a literary tradition. The collective publication of these works by black women now, for the first time, makes it possible for scholars and critics, male and female, black and white, to *demonstrate* that black women writers read, and revised, other black women writers. To demonstrate this set of formal literary relations is to demonstrate that sexuality, race, and gender are both the condition and the basis of *tradition*—but tradition as found in discrete acts of language use.

A word is in order about the history of this set. For the past decade, I have taught a course, first at Yale and then at Cornell, entitled "Black Women and Their Fictions," a course that I inherited from Toni Morrison, who developed it in the mid-1970s for Yale's Program in Afro-American Studies. Although the course was inspired by the remarkable accomplishments of black women novelists since 1970, I gradually extended its beginning date to the late nineteenth century, studying Frances Harper's *Iola Leroy* and Anna Julia Cooper's *A Voice From the South*, both published in 1892. With the discovery of Harriet E. Wilson's seminal novel, *Our Nig* (1859), and Jean Yellin's authentication of Harriet Jacobs's brilliant slave narrative, *Incidents in the Life of a Slave Girl* (1861), a survey course spanning over a century and a quarter emerged.

But the discovery of *Our Nig*, as well as the interest in nineteenth-century black women's writing that this discovery generated, convinced me that even the most curious and diligent scholars knew very little of the extensive history of the creative writings of Afro-American women before 1900. Indeed, most scholars of Afro-American literature had never even read most of the books published by black women, simply because these books—of poetry, novels, short stories, essays, and autobiography—were mostly accessible only in rare book sections of university libraries. For reasons unclear to me even today, few of these marvelous renderings of the Afro American woman's consciousness were reprinted in the late 1960s and early 1970s, when so many other texts of the Afro-American literary tradition were resurrected from the dark and silent graveyard of the out-of-print and were reissued in facsimile editions aimed at the hungry readership for canonical texts in the nascent field of black studies.

So, with the help of several superb research assistants—including David Curtis, Nicola Shilliam, Wendy Jones, Sam Otter, Janadas Devan, Suvir Kaul, Cynthia Bond, Elizabeth Alexander, and Adele Alexander—and with the expert advice of scholars such as William Robinson, William Andrews, Mary Helen Washington, Maryemma Graham, Jean Yellin, Houston A. Baker, Jr., Richard Yarborough, Hazel Carby, Joan R. Sherman, Frances Foster, and William French, dozens of bibliographies were used to compile a list of books written or narrated by black women mostly before 1910. Without the assistance provided through this shared experience of scholarship, the scholar's true legacy, this project could not have been conceived. As the list grew, I was struck by how very many of these titles that I, for example, had never even heard of, let alone read, such as Ann Plato's *Essays,* Louisa Picquet's slave narrative, or Amelia Johnson's two novels, *Clarence and Corinne* and *The Hazeley Family.* Through our research with the Black Periodical Fiction and Poetry Project (funded by NEH and the Ford Foundation), I also realized that several novels by black women, including three works of fiction by Pauline Hopkins, had been serialized in black periodicals, but had never been collected and published as books. Nor had the several books of poetry published by black women, such as the prolific Frances E. W. Harper, been collected and edited. When I discovered still another "lost" novel by an Afro-American woman (*Four Girls at Cottage City,* published in 1898 by Emma Dunham Kelley-Hawkins), I decided to attempt to edit a collection of reprints of these works and to publish them as a "library" of black women's writings, in part so that I could read them myself.

Convincing university and trade publishers to undertake this project proved to be a difficult task. Despite the commercial success of *Our Nig* and of the several reprint series of women's works (such as Virago, the Beacon Black Women Writers Series, and Rutgers' American Women Writers Series), several presses rejected the project as "too large," "too limited," or as "commercially unviable." Only two publishers recognized the viability and the import of the project and, of these, Oxford's commitment to publish the titles simultaneously as a set made the press's offer irresistible.

While attempting to locate original copies of these exceedingly rare books, I discovered that most of the texts were housed at the Schomburg Center for Research in Black Culture, a branch of The New York Public Library, under the direction of Howard Dodson. Dodson's infectious enthusiasm for the project and his generous collaboration, as well as that of his stellar staff (especially Diana Lachatanere, Sharon Howard, Ellis Haizip, Richard Newman, and Betty Gubert), led to a joint publishing initiative that produced this set as part of the Schomburg's major fund-raising campaign. Without Dodson's foresight and generosity of spirit, the set would not have materialized. Without William P. Sisler's masterful editorship at Oxford and his staff's careful attention to detail, the set would have remained just another grand idea that tends to languish in a scholar's file cabinet.

I would also like to thank Dr. Michael Winston and Dr. Thomas C. Battle, Vice-President of Academic Affairs and the Director of the Moorland-Spingarn Research Center (respectively) at Howard University, for their unending encouragement, support, and collaboration in this project, and Esme E. Bhan at Howard for her meticulous research and bibliographical skills. In addition, I would like to acknowledge the aid of the staff at the libraries of Duke University, Cornell University (especially Tom Weissinger and Donald Eddy), the Boston Public Library, the Western Reserve Historical Society, the Library of Congress, and Yale University. Linda Robbins, Marion Osmun, Sarah Flanagan, and Gerard Case, all members of the staff at Oxford, were extraordinarily effective at coordinating, editing, and producing the various segments of each text in the set. Candy Ruck, Nina de Tar, and Phillis Molock expertly typed reams of correspondence and manuscripts connected to the project.

I would also like to express my gratitude to my colleagues who edited and introduced the individual titles in the set. Without their attention to detail, their willingness to meet strict deadlines, and their sheer enthusiasm for this project, the set could not have been published. But finally and ultimately, I would hope that the publication of the set would help to generate even more scholarly interest in the black women authors whose work is presented here. Struggling against the seemingly insurmountable barriers of racism *and* sexism, while often raising families and fulfilling full-time professional obligations, these women managed nevertheless to record their thoughts and feelings and to *testify* to all who dare read them that the will to harness the power of collective endurance and survival is the will to write.

The Schomburg Library of Nineteenth-Century Black Women Writers is dedicated in memory of Pauline Augusta Coleman Gates, who died in the spring of 1987. It was she who inspired in me the love of learning and the love of literature. I have encountered in the books of this set no will more determined, no courage more noble, no mind more sublime, no self more celebratory of the achievements of all Afro-American women, and indeed of life itself, than her own.

# A NOTE FROM
# THE SCHOMBURG CENTER

*Howard Dodson*

The Schomburg Center for Research in Black Culture, The New York Public Library, is pleased to join with Dr. Henry Louis Gates and Oxford University Press in presenting The Schomburg Library of Nineteenth-Century Black Women Writers. This thirty-volume set includes the work of a generation of black women whose writing has only been available previously in rare book collections. The materials reprinted in twenty-four of the thirty volumes are drawn from the unique holdings of the Schomburg Center.

A research unit of The New York Public Library, the Schomburg Center has been in the forefront of those institutions dedicated to collecting, preserving, and providing access to the records of the black past. In the course of its two generations of acquisition and conservation activity, the Center has amassed collections totaling more than 5 million items. They include over 100,000 bound volumes, 85,000 reels and sets of microforms, 300 manuscript collections containing some 3.5 million items, 300,000 photographs and extensive holdings of prints, sound recordings, film and videotape, newspapers, artworks, artifacts, and other book and nonbook materials. Together they vividly document the history and cultural heritages of people of African descent worldwide.

Though established some sixty-two years ago, the Center's book collections date from the sixteenth century. Its oldest item, an Ethiopian Coptic Tunic, dates from the eighth or ninth century. Rare materials, however, are most available for the nineteenth-century African-American experience. It is from these holdings that the majority of the titles selected for inclusion in this set are drawn.

The nineteenth century was a formative period in African-American literary and cultural history. Prior to the Civil War, the majority of black Americans living in the United States were held in bondage. Law and practice forbade teaching them to read or write. Even after the war, many of the impediments to learning and literary productivity remained. Nevertheless, black men and women of the nineteenth century persevered in both areas. Moreover, more African-Americans than we yet realize turned their observations, feelings, social viewpoints, and creative impulses into published works. In time, this nineteenth-century printed record included poetry, short stories, histories, novels, autobiographies, social criticism, and theology, as well as economic and philosophical treatises. Unfortunately, much of this body of literature remained, until very recently, relatively inaccessible to twentieth-century scholars, teachers, creative artists, and others interested in black life. Prior to the late 1960s, most Americans (black as well as white) had never heard of these nineteenth-century authors, much less read their works.

The civil rights and black power movements created unprecedented interest in the thought, behavior, and achievements of black people. Publishers responded by revising traditional texts, introducing the American public to a new generation of African-American writers, publishing a variety of thematic anthologies, and reprinting a plethora of "classic texts" in African-American history, literature, and art. The reprints usually appeared as individual titles or in a series of bound volumes or microform formats.

The Schomburg Center, which has a long history of supporting publishing that deals with the history and culture of Africans in diaspora, became an active participant in many of the reprint revivals of the 1960s. Since hard copies of original printed works are the preferred formats for producing facsimile reproductions, publishers frequently turned to the Schomburg Center for copies of these original titles. In addition to providing such material, Schomburg Center staff members offered advice and consultation, wrote introductions, and occasionally entered into formal copublishing arrangements in some projects.

Most of the nineteenth-century titles reprinted during the 1960s, however, were by and about black men. A few black women were included in the longer series, but works by lesser known black women were generally overlooked. The Schomburg Library of Nineteenth-Century Black Women Writers is both a corrective to these previous omissions and an important contribution to Afro-American literary history in its own right. Through this collection of volumes, the thoughts, perspectives, and creative abilities of nineteenth-century African-American women, as captured in books and pamphlets published in large part before 1910, are again being made available to the general public. The Schomburg Center is pleased to be a part of this historic endeavor.

I would like to thank Professor Gates for initiating this project. Thanks are due both to him and Mr. William P. Sisler of Oxford University Press for giving the Schomburg Center an opportunity to play such a prominent role in the set. Thanks are also due to my colleagues at The New York Public Library and the Schomburg Center, especially Dr. Vartan Gregorian, Richard De Gennaro, Paul Fasana, Betsy

Pinover, Richard Newman, Diana Lachatanere, Glenderlyn Johnson, and Harold Anderson for their assistance and support. I can think of no better way of demonstrating than in this set the role the Schomburg Center plays in assuring that the black heritage will be available for future generations.

# INTRODUCTION

*William L. Andrews*

No autobiography by an Afro-American woman of the nineteenth century defies classification more than *Wonderful Adventures of Mrs. Seacole in Many Lands* (1857). A free-born Jamaican, evidently well protected from the tentacles of slavery, Mary Jane Grant Seacole did not write her narrative expressly to advance the cause of antislavery, as so many Afro-American women autobiographers did during her era. Twenty-five years before she gave her story to the public, slavery had been abolished in the British Empire. Thus to obtain an intimate view of slavery in the British West Indies, one must consult the chilling *History of Mary Prince, a West Indian Slave* (1831), not the recollections of Mrs. Seacole. Seacole's admiration for the bravery and enterprise of ex-slaves appears repeatedly in her story, and her contempt for slaveowners provides her sarcasm a ready target, but one does not read her autobiography as part of the slave narrative tradition.

The experience of a free black woman in Jamaica in the 1840s is recounted in *A Narrative of the Life and Travels of Mrs. Nancy Prince* (1850) as well as in Seacole's autobiography. But Prince found Jamaica so "blinded to every thing but money" and so tense on the racial front that she felt compelled to build her missionary career anew in the United States. By contrast, Seacole's Jamaica provides opportunity for a "hearty, strong woman" like herself to "succeed in life," and succeed she does, first as a storekeeper and later as a self-supporting widow specializing in treating the ills of British officers stationed in Kingston. Nancy Gardner Prince, like

most spiritual autobiographers in the Christian tradition,
summed up her story by warning that "fearful indeed is the
world's pilgrimage" apart from a saving dependence on God.
Mary Seacole knew much about worldly struggle and tribu-
lation, but she did not conclude, with Nancy Prince, that life
was "fearful," nor did she treat her experience as a means of
thanking God for all He had done to protect her from evil.
Far from irreligious, Seacole believed that her work as a
battlefield "doctress" in the Crimean War was completely in
the spirit of Christian charity. Still, her interpretation of a
black woman's international adventures is more self-revealing
and less divinely oriented—in a word, more secular—than is
Nancy Prince's. Seacole's urbanity and cosmopolitan wit, along
with her indomitable spirit and frankness about her own foi-
bles, make her narrative one of the most readable and rewarding black women's autobiographies of the nineteenth
century.

Seacole has little to say about her childhood in Kingston,
Jamaica, but what she does bring out is designed to explain
and justify her temperament and the motives that molded her
destiny. A Creole, born of a Scottish army officer and a free
black boardinghouse keeper, Seacole emphasizes her "good
Scotch blood" as determining her unceasing desire "to be up
and doing" in good white Western fashion. Though she is at
pains to distinguish herself from the "lazy Creole" stereotype
prevalent in the thinking of whites in her homeland, she does
not fail to credit her mother with having passed on a talent
for herbal medicine and a "yearning for medical knowledge
and practice which has never deserted me." Combining the
heritage of mother and father, Seacole acknowledges an "ambition to become a doctress" that is only briefly sidetracked
by her marriage. After paying proper respect to the ephem-

eral Mr. Seacole, she devotes the rest of her account of her
early years to a description of her powerful desire "to succeed
in life" and the means by which she aimed to gratify that
desire. Readers of today will be impressed by her nondomes-
tic zest for roaming and her resolution to support herself as
"an unprotected female," in other words, as a widow, rather
than take a second husband in a bid for economic security.
This work, then, besides being an adventure narrative, is a
special kind of success story in which a woman tries to rec-
oncile her desire for economic independence and worldly recognition with a more socially acceptable role of being properly selfless and useful to men. "I love to be of service to
those who need a woman's help," she explains early in her
story. But she sees no reason why she should not be "pleased
and gratified" emotionally and financially by her services, and
though she knows that she will be considered by some to be
"vain and egotistical," she feels no qualms about acknowl-
edging her personal pride in her accomplishments.

Seacole's quest for personal fulfillment through a useful
occupation began in Panama during the early 1850s, where
she went to help manage her brother's hotel and store in
Cruces, a point of transit for prospectors from the United
States heading to or from the California goldfields. The
physical hardships that she encountered in crossing the Isthmus and living in Cruces are presented in her autobiography
in realistic, sometimes almost sordid, detail. Her picture of
life in a Central American frontier town, where extreme wealth
and poverty are mixed in a volatile, multiracial setting, dis-
plays not only Seacole's narrative gifts, but her urbane sense
of humor as well. Her portrait of the proverbial "ugly
American" is particularly striking due to her sensitivity to
the racial as well as national chauvinism of those she lumps

together as "the Yankees." No doubt the Southerners whom she labeled with this misnomer would have been greatly incensed, but those from the North would also have been stung by her criticism of "the airs of superiority which many Americans have endeavoured to assume over me." With her typical frankness, Seacole confesses to "a little prejudice" against all North Americans because of the complicity of the entire United States in the institution of slavery. Yet she is quick to point out that her impressions are based on only a partial sample—namely, the California gold seekers—and that she has met some "delightful exceptions" to the American type.

In Seacole's hands, American boorishness, obtuseness, bigotry, and arrogance all come to life in memorable caricatures, both male and female. From her description of American table manners to her story of the comeuppance of a female slaveowner at the hands of a local black *alcalde* (chief magistrate), Seacole's irony does exquisite justice to "these free and independent filibusters, who would fain whop all creation abroad as they do their slaves at home." An excellent example of her satirical talent is her rendition, in dialect, of a fulsome toast to "Aunty Seacole, the best yaller woman [God] ever made," as delivered by a pompous tobacco-chewing Southerner. Seacole claims to have had her revenge on such people both verbally (as in her reply to the Southerner's toast) and monetarily ("I made money out of their wants"). Nevertheless, the persistent annoyance, if not outrage, of having to endure the many slights and slurs of the Americans, coupled with the rigors of frontier living, seem to have exhausted her yen for adventure in Panama. She returned to Jamaica in 1853 disgusted with Yankees and "the Spanish Indians," but deeply respectful of the black people of New Granada (now Panama and Colombia), many of whom, she observes, were escaped slaves from the United States. "Whatever was of any worth in [New Granada's] institutions, such as their comparative freedom, religious toleration, etc., was owing mainly to the negroes who had sought the protection of the republic."

After several months of aimless activity, Seacole was thrilled to learn of the outbreak of the Crimean War and Britain's entry into the war in the spring of 1854. "No sooner had I heard of war somewhere, than I longed to witness it; and when I was told that many of the regiments I had known so well in Jamaica had left England for the scene of action, the desire to join them became stronger than ever." Every possible obstacle was put between her and her Crimean destination, but the black woman overcame them all. Upon her arrival in Balaclava in the winter of 1855, she set about establishing her "British Hotel," replete with a store, a canteen for enlisted men, a kitchen and small mess hall for officers, and a medical dispensary and sick bay. The fame of Mrs. Seacole spread throughout the British front not only because of the amenities offered by her hotel but also because of her skill as a nurse and doctress. Although she introduces her reader to the war in comic fashion by recounting her dealings with Greek and Maltese thieves, Crimean rats, a Falstaffian Turkish Pacha, and a wayward English pig, she reserves a few chapters for more sober matters of war, of which she learned firsthand through her nursing work. Seacole knows how to communicate in graphic human terms the horrors and misery of battle, and some of the deathbed vignettes she recounts are genuinely touching. Yet it is hard not to conclude from her narrative that she felt quite at home in a war environment and was not a little disappointed when the armistice was signed in 1856. Although the experience of battle and the loss of many of her "sons" took a terrible toll, "Mother Seacole" had to admit that "I do not pray God that I may never see its like again," for "I wish to be useful all my life, and it is in scenes of horror and distress that a woman can do so much."

Returning to England put Seacole in the public eye as just the sort of "Crimean *heroine*" she had set out to become. Her narrative ends with her savoring her recollections of the friendships she made with the famous and the common men of the army. Despite her financial sacrifices, Seacole maintains her stiff upper lip in the conclusion to her *Wonderful Adventures,* stressing not her loss of health and fortune but her gains, especially in the eyes of those who called her "mother" and made her their symbol of all they treasured at home. For these men, the end of the war came as a great relief, since it meant they could return to the home they had left. But for Seacole, the end of the conflict meant separation, not reunion, and she could not conceal from her reader the strong ambivalence she felt about her own return to England. "All this going home seemed strange and somewhat sad, and sometimes I felt that I could not sympathise with the glad faces and happy hearts of those who were looking forward to the delights of home." Seacole felt more "fellow-feeling" with those who had entered the army "by choice and necessity" because they had no home and because action gave them "excitement, occupation, the chance of promotion." She too had been "happy through the months of toil and danger, never knowing what fear or depression was, finding every moment of the day mortgaged hours in advance." And so, the self-styled heroine of the Crimea left the front with the ominous sense of "how likely was it that my present occupation gone, I might long in vain for another so stirring and so useful."

Students of Seacole's biography report that her friends in England tried through various fund-raising efforts to help restore her to financial solvency, but with little success. It is likely that she wrote her autobiography a year after her return to England in order to capitalize as best she could on her brief prominence in the public eye. After this, the fifty-two-year-old Seacole involved herself in the cause of war widows and orphans. As the years went by, many men who felt indebted to her ministrations in the Crimea visited her apartment in London's West End, and she was decorated by the French, Turkish, and probably the English governments for her service during the war. During the 1870s she cultivated a friendship with the Princess of Wales, for whom she evidently worked as a masseuse. Mary Seacole died in prosperous circumstances on May 14, 1881, and was buried in St. Mary's Catholic Cemetery in London. (For useful historical and biographical information on Seacole and her autobiography, see *Wonderful Adventures of Mrs. Seacole in Many Lands*, ed. Ziggi Alexander and Audrey Dewjee [Bristol, England: Falling Wall Press, 1984], pp. 9–45.)

The life of Mary Jane Grant Seacole was "wonderful" and successful in many respects. If her autobiography presents her experience in these terms, with little false modesty and a fair share of name-dropping, we should remember that Seacole had little patience with pretense of any sort, preferring instead to treat her reader "in a friendly confidential way" that let her speak her mind. Perhaps it is her willingness to "confess" to feelings that many women of her time, white or black, would have concealed that helps to make her autobiography so attractive.

Seacole insists from the outset of her story that her experience of the world "leads me to the conclusion that it is by no means the hard bad world which some selfish people would

have us believe it." That this black woman could hold onto
such Victorian optimism is no small testimony to the "confidence in [her] own powers" that she claims as hers from
youth. Yet beneath the buoyancy of the *Wonderful Adventures*
we can also detect an undercurrent of a longing unfulfilled
for a home where a black woman could feel perpetually useful, needed, and loved. On the Crimean front, in the midst
of so many needy "sons," Seacole seems to have created for
herself, at least temporarily, a social identity and a sense of
community sustaining to *her* needs. In the Crimea she became "Mother" Seacole, not the sentimentalized black "Aunty"
of condescending white American imagination, but an independent and highly respected maternal figure, the acme of
female achievement in Victorian culture, the symbol of all
that "home" signified to British soldiers alienated by war.
Was Seacole aware of the pathetic irony of her situation,
namely, that she found home only when war had sundered
the homes of her beloved "sons"? Did she feel the poignancy
of her peculiar motherhood, which war made possible even
as it bereaved so many mothers of their sons? Did she see
these ironies as a commentary on her condition as a black
woman trying assiduously to make a respectable place for
herself in the Western scheme of things? Tantalizing ambi-
guities such as these make Mrs. Seacole a fascinating figure
and her *Wonderful Adventures* a stimulating reading experience from beginning to end.

Wonderful Adventures of
Mrs. Seacole in Many Lands

MRS. SEACOLE'S HOTEL IN THE CRIMEA.

WONDERFUL

# ADVENTURES OF MRS. SEACOLE

## IN MANY LANDS.

EDITED BY W. J. S.

———◆———

WITH AN INTRODUCTORY PREFACE

BY

W. H. RUSSELL, ESQ.,

THE "TIMES" CORRESPONDENT IN THE CRIMEA.

———◆———

LONDON:

JAMES BLACKWOOD, PATERNOSTER ROW.

1857.

LONDON :

THOMAS HARRILD, PRINTER, 11, SALISBURY SQUARE,
FLEET STREET.

# TO THE READER.

—◆—

I should have thought that no preface would have been required to introduce Mrs. Seacole to the British public, or to recommend a book which must, from the circumstances in which the subject of it was placed, be unique in literature.

If singleness of heart, true charity, and Christian works; if trials and sufferings, dangers and perils, encountered boldly by a helpless woman on her errand of mercy in the camp and in the battle-field, can excite sympathy or move curiosity, Mary Seacole will have many friends and many readers.

She is no Anna Comnena, who presents us with a verbose history, but a plain truth-speaking woman, who has lived an adventurous life amid scenes which have never yet found a historian among the actors on the stage where they passed.

I have witnessed her devotion and her courage; I have already borne testimony to her services to all who needed them. She is the first who has redeemed the name of "sutler" from the suspicion of worthlessness, mercenary baseness, and plunder; and I trust that England will not forget one who nursed her sick, who sought out her wounded to aid and succour them, and who performed the last offices for some of her illustrious dead.

W. H. RUSSELL.

# CONTENTS.

———◆———

## CHAPTER VI.

## CHAPTER VII.

## CHAPTER VIII.

## CHAPTER IX.

## CHAPTER X.

### CHAPTER XI.

### CHAPTER XII.

### CHAPTER XIII.

### CHAPTER XIV.

### CHAPTER XV.

### CHAPTER XVI.

## CHAPTER XVII.

## CHAPTER XVIII.

## CHAPTER XIX.

# ADVENTURES OF MRS. SEACOLE

## IN MANY LANDS.

———◆———

### CHAPTER I.

MY BIRTH AND PARENTAGE—EARLY TASTES AND TRAVELS—
MARRIAGE, AND WIDOWHOOD.

I WAS born in the town of Kingston, in the island of
Jamaica, some time in the present century. As a female,
and a widow, I may be well excused giving the precise
date of this important event. But I do not mind confessing that the century and myself were both young together,
and that we have grown side by side into age and consequence. I am a Creole, and have good Scotch blood
coursing in my veins. My father was a soldier, of an old
Scotch family; and to him I often trace my affection for a
camp-life, and my sympathy with what I have heard my
friends call "the pomp, pride, and circumstance of glorious
war." Many people have also traced to my Scotch blood
that energy and activity which are not always found in
the Creole race, and which have carried me to so many

B

varied scenes: and perhaps they are right. I have often
heard the term "lazy Creole" applied to my country people;
but I am sure I do not know what it is to be indolent. All
my life long I have followed the impulse which led me to
be up and doing; and so far from resting idle anywhere, I
have never wanted inclination to rove, nor will powerful
enough to find a way to carry out my wishes. That these
qualities have led me into many countries, and brought me
into some strange and amusing adventures, the reader, if
he or she has the patience to get through this book, will
see. Some people, indeed, have called me quite a female
Ulysses. I believe that they intended it as a compliment;
but from my experience of the Greeks, I do not consider it
a very flattering one.

It is not my intention to dwell at any length upon the
recollections of my childhood. My mother kept a boardinghouse in Kingston, and was, like very many of the Creole
women, an admirable doctress; in high repute with the
officers of both services, and their wives, who were from
time to time stationed at Kingston. It was very natural
that I should inherit her tastes; and so I had from early
youth a yearning for medical knowledge and practice which
has never deserted me. When I was a very young child I
was taken by an old lady, who brought me up in her
household among her own grandchildren, and who could
scarcely have shown me more kindness had I been one of
them; indeed, I was so spoiled by my kind patroness that,
but for being frequently with my mother, I might very
likely have grown up idle and useless. But I saw so much
of her, and of her patients, that the ambition to become a
doctress early took firm root in my mind; and I was very

young when I began to make use of the little knowledge
I had acquired from watching my mother, upon a great
sufferer—my doll. I have noticed always what actors
children are. If you leave one alone in a room, how soon
it clears a little stage; and, making an audience out of a
few chairs and stools, proceeds to act its childish griefs and
blandishments upon its doll. So I also made good use of
my dumb companion and confidante; and whatever disease
was most prevalent in Kingston, be sure my poor doll soon
contracted it. I have had many medical triumphs in later
days, and saved some valuable lives; but I really think
that few have given me more real gratification than the
rewarding glow of health which my fancy used to picture
stealing over my patient's waxen face after long and pre-
carious illness.

Before long it was very natural that I should seek to
extend my practice; and so I found other patients in the
dogs and cats around me. Many luckless brutes were
made to simulate diseases which were raging among their
owners, and had forced down their reluctant throats the
remedies which I deemed most likely to suit their supposed
complaints. And after a time I rose still higher in my
ambition; and despairing of finding another human patient, I proceeded to try my simples and essences upon—
myself.

When I was about twelve years old I was more frequently at my mother's house, and used to assist her in her
duties; very often sharing with her the task of attendin
upon invalid officers or their wives, who came to her house
from the adjacent camp at Up-Park, or the military station
at Newcastle.

As I grew into womanhood, I began to indulge that
longing to travel which will never leave me while I have
health and vigour.   I was never weary of tracing upon an
old map the route to England; and never followed with my
gaze the stately ships homeward bound without longing to
be in them, and see the blue hills of Jamaica fade into the
distance.   At that time it seemed most improbable that
these girlish wishes should be gratified; but circumstances,
which I need not explain, enabled me to accompany some
relatives to England while I was yet a very young woman.

I shall never forget my first impressions of London.
Of course, I am not going to bore the reader with them;
but they are as vivid now as though the year 18— (I had
very nearly let my age slip then) had not been long ago
numbered with the past.   Strangely enough, some of the
most vivid of my recollections are the efforts of the London
street-boys to poke fun at my and my companion's complexion.   I am only a little brown—a few shades duskier
than the brunettes whom you all admire so much; but my
companion was very dark, and a fair (if I can apply the
term to her) subject for their rude wit.   She was hot-
tempered, poor thing! and as there were no policemen to
awe the boys and turn our servants' heads in those days,
our progress through the London streets was sometimes a
rather chequered one.

I remained in England, upon the occasion of my first
visit, about a year; and then returned to Kingston.   Before
long I again started for London, bringing with me this
time a large stock of West Indian preserves and pickles for
sale.   After remaining two years here, I again started
home; and on the way my life and adventures were very

nearly brought to a premature conclusion. Christmas-day had been kept very merrily on board our ship the "Velusia;" and on the following day a fire broke out in the hold. I dare say it would have resisted all the crew's efforts to put it out, had not another ship appeared in sight; upon which the fire quietly allowed itself to be extinguished. Although considerably alarmed, I did not lose my senses; but during the time when the contest between fire and water was doubtful, I entered into an amicable arrangement with the ship's cook, whereby, in consideration of two pounds— which I was not, however, to pay until the crisis arrived— he agreed to lash me on to a large hen-coop.

Before I had been long in Jamaica I started upon other trips, many of them undertaken with a view to gain. Thus I spent some time in New Providence, bringing home with me a large collection of handsome shells and rare shell-work, which created quite a sensation in Kingston, and had a rapid sale; I visited also Hayti and Cuba. But I hasten onward in my narrative.

Returned to Kingston, I nursed my old indulgent patroness in her last long illness. After she died, in my arms, I went to my mother's house, where I stayed, making myself useful in a variety of ways, and learning a great deal of Creole medicinal art, until I couldn't find courage to say "no" to a certain arrangement timidly proposed by Mr. Seacole, but married him, and took him down to Black River, where we established a store. Poor man! he was very delicate; and before I undertook the charge of him, several doctors had expressed most unfavourable opinions of his health. I kept him alive by kind nursing and attention as long as I could; but at last he

grew so ill that we left Black River, and returned to my
mother's house at Kingston. Within a month of our arrival there he died. This was my first great trouble, and I felt
it bitterly. For days I never stirred—lost to all that passed
around me in a dull stupor of despair. If you had told me
that the time would soon come when I should remember
this sorrow calmly, I should not have believed it possible:
and yet it was so. I do not think that we hot-blooded
Creoles sorrow less for showing it so impetuously; but I
do think that the sharp edge of our grief wears down
sooner than theirs who preserve an outward demeanour of
calmness, and nurse their woe secretly in their hearts.

## CHAPTER II.

STRUGGLES FOR LIFE—THE CHOLERA IN JAMAICA—I LEAVE KINGS-
TON FOR THE ISTHMUS OF PANAMA—CHAGRES, NAVY BAY, AND
GATUN—LIFE IN PANAMA—UP THE RIVER CHAGRES TO GORGONA
AND CRUCES.

I HAD one other great grief to master—the loss of my
mother, and then I was left alone to battle with the world
as best I might. The struggles which it cost me to succeed in life were sometimes very trying; nor have they
ended yet. But I have always turned a bold front to fortune, and taken, and shall continue to take, as my brave
friends in the army and navy have shown me how, "my
hurts before." Although it was no easy thing for a
widow to make ends meet, I never allowed myself to know

what repining or depression was, and so succeeded in gaining not only my daily bread, but many comforts besides, from the beginning. Indeed, my experience of the world —it is not finished yet, but I do not think it will give me reason to change my opinion—leads me to the conclusion that it is by no means the hard bad world which some selfish people would have us believe it. It may be as my editor says —

> "That gently comes the world to those
> That are cast in gentle mould;"

hinting at the same time, politely, that the rule may apply to me personally. And perhaps he is right, for although I was always a hearty, strong woman—plain-spoken people might say stout—I think my heart is soft enough.

How slowly and gradually I succeeded in life, need not be told at length. My fortunes underwent the variations which befall all. Sometimes I was rich one day, and poor the next. I never thought too exclusively of money, believing rather that we were born to be happy, and that the surest way to be wretched is to prize it over-much. Had I done so, I should have mourned over many a promising speculation proving a failure, over many a pan of preserves or guava jelly burnt in the making; and perhaps lost my mind when the great fire of 1843, which devastated Kingston, burnt down my poor home. As it was, I very nearly lost my life, for I would not leave my house until every chance of saving it had gone, and it was wrapped in flames. But, of course, I set to work again in a humbler way, and rebuilt my house by degrees, and restocked it, succeeding better than before; for I had gained a reputation as a skilful nurse and doctress, and my house

was always full of invalid officers and their wives from
Newcastle, or the adjacent Up-Park Camp. Sometimes I
had a naval or military surgeon under my roof, from whom
I never failed to glean instruction, given, when they learned
my love for their profession, with a readiness and kindness I am never likely to forget. Many of these kind
friends are alive now. I met with some when my adventures had carried me to the battle-fields of the Crimea; and
to those whose eyes may rest upon these pages I again
offer my acknowledgments for their past kindness, which
helped me to be useful to my kind in many lands.

And here I may take the opportunity of explaining
that it was from a confidence in my own powers, and not
at all from necessity, that I remained an unprotected female.
Indeed, I do not mind confessing to my reader, in a friendly
confidential way, that one of the hardest struggles of my
life in Kingston was to resist the pressing candidates for
the late Mr. Seacole's shoes.

Officers of high rank sometimes took up their abode in
my house. Others of inferior rank were familiar with me,
long before their bravery, and, alas! too often death, in
the Crimea, made them world famous. There were few
officers of the 97th to whom Mother Seacole was not well
known, before she joined them in front of Sebastopol; and
among the best known was good-hearted, loveable, noble
H—— V——, whose death shocked me so terribly, and
with whose useful heroic life the English public have become so familiar. I can hear the ring of his boyish laughter even now.

In the year 1850, the cholera swept over the island of
Jamaica with terrible force. Our idea—perhaps an un-

founded one—was, that a steamer from New Orleans was the means of introducing it into the island. Anyhow, they sent some clothes on shore to be washed, and poor Dolly Johnson, the washerwoman, whom we all knew, sickened and died of the terrible disease. While the cholera raged, I had but too many opportunities of watching its nature, and from a Dr. B——, who was then lodging in my house, received many hints as to its treatment which I afterwards found invaluable.

Early in the same year my brother had left Kingston for the Isthmus of Panama, then the great high-road to and from golden California, where he had established a considerable store and hotel. Ever since he had done so, I had found some difficulty in checking my reviving disposition to roam, and at last persuading myself that I might be of use to him (he was far from strong), I resigned my house into the hands of a cousin, and made arrangements to journey to Chagres. Having come to this conclusion, I allowed no grass to grow beneath my feet, but set to work busily, for I was not going to him empty-handed. My house was full for weeks, of tailors, making up rough coats, trousers, etc., and sempstresses cutting out and making shirts. In addition to these, my kitchen was filled with busy people, manufacturing preserves, guava jelly, and other delicacies, while a considerable sum was invested in the purchase of preserved meats, vegetables, and eggs. It will be as well, perhaps, if I explain, in as few words as possible, the then condition of the Isthmus of Panama.

All my readers must know—a glance at the map will show it to those who do not—that between North America and the envied shores of California stretches a little neck of land, insignificant-looking enough on the map, dividing the Atlantic from the Pacific.  By crossing this, the travellers from America avoided a long, weary, and dangerous sea voyage round Cape Horn, or an almost impossible journey by land.

But that journey across the Isthmus, insignificant in distance as it was, was by no means an easy one.  It seemed as if nature had determined to throw every conceivable obstacle in the way of those who should seek to join the two great oceans of the world.  I have read and heard many accounts of old endeavours to effect this important and gigantic work, and how miserably they failed.  It was reserved for the men of our age to accomplish what so many had died in attempting, and iron and steam, twin giants, subdued to man's will, have put a girdle over rocks and rivers, so that travellers can glide as smoothly, if not as inexpensively, over the once terrible Isthmus of Darien, as they can from London to Brighton.  Not yet, however, does civilization rule at Panama.  The weak sway of the New Granada Republic, despised by lawless men, and respected by none, is powerless to control the refuse of every nation which meet together upon its soil.  Whenever they feel inclined now they overpower the law easily; but seven years ago, when I visited the Isthmus of Panama, things were much worse, and a licence existed, compared to which the present lawless state of affairs is enviable.

When, after passing Chagres, an old-world, tumble-down town, for about seven miles, the steamer reached Navy Bay, I thought I had never seen a more luckless, dreary spot.  Three sides of the place were a mere swamp, and the town itself stood upon a sand-reef, the houses being built upon piles, which some one told me rotted regularly every three years. The railway, which now connects the bay with Panama, was then building, and ran, as far as we could see, on piles, connected with the town by a wooden jetty. It seemed as capital a nursery for ague and fever as Death could hit upon anywhere, and those on board the steamer who knew it confirmed my opinion. As we arrived a steady down-pour of rain was falling from an inky sky; the white men who met us on the wharf appeared ghostly and wraith-like, and the very negroes seemed pale and wan. The news which met us did not tempt me to lose any time in getting up the country to my brother. According to all accounts, fever and ague, with some minor diseases, especially dropsy, were having it all their own way at Navy Bay, and, although I only stayed one night in the place, my medicine chest was called into requisition. But the sufferers wanted remedies which I could not give them—warmth, nourishment, and fresh air Beneath leaky tents, damp huts, and even under broken railway waggons, I saw men dying from sheer exhaustion Indeed, I was very glad when, with the morning, the crowd, as the Yankees called the bands of pilgrims to and from California, made ready to ascend to Panama.

The first stage of our journey was by railway to Gatun, about twelve miles distant. For the greater portion of that distance the lines ran on piles, over as unhealthy and wretched a country as the eye could well grow weary of; but, at last, the country improved, and you caught glimpses of distant hills and English-like scenery. Every mile of that fatal railway cost the world thousands of lives. I was assured that its site was marked thickly by graves, and that so great was the mortality among the labourers that three times the survivors struck in a body, and their places had to be supplied by fresh victims from America, tempted by unheard-of rates of wages. It is a gigantic undertaking, and shows what the energy and enterprise of man can accomplish. Everything requisite for its construction, even the timber, had to be prepared in, and brought from, America.

The railway then ran no further than Gatun, and here we were to take water and ascend the River Chagres to Gorgona, the next stage on the way to Cruces, where my brother was. The cars landed us at the bottom of a somewhat steep cutting through a reddish clay, and deposited me and my suite, consisting of a black servant, named "Mac," and a little girl, in safety in the midst of my many packages, not altogether satisfied with my prospects; for the rain was falling heavily and steadily, and the Gatun porters were possessing themselves of my luggage with that same avidity which distinguishes their brethren on the pier of Calais or the quays of Pera. There are two species of individuals whom I have found alike wherever my travels have carried me—the reader can guess their professions—porters and lawyers.

It was as much as I could do to gather my packages together, sit in the midst with a determined look to awe the hungry crowd around me, and send "Mac" up the steep slippery bank to report progress. After a little while he returned to say that the river-side was not far off, where boats could be hired for the upward journey. The word given, the porters threw themselves upon my packages; a pitched battle ensued, out of which issued the strongest

Spanish Indians, with their hardly earned prizes, and we commenced the ascent of the clayey bank. Now, although the surveyors of the Darien highways had considerately cut steps up the steep incline, they had become worse than useless, so I floundered about terribly, more than once losing my footing altogether. And as with that due regard to personal appearance, which I have always deemed a duty as well as a pleasure to study, I had, before leaving Navy Bay, attired myself in a delicate light blue dress, a white bonnet prettily trimmed, and an equally chaste shawl, the reader can sympathise with my distress. However, I gained the summit, and after an arduous descent, of a few minutes duration, reached the river-side; in a most piteous plight, however, for my pretty dress, from its contact with the Gatun clay, looked as red as if, in the pursuit of science, I had passed it through a strong solution of muriatic acid.

By the water-side I found my travelling companions arguing angrily with the shrewd boatmen, and bating down their fares. Upon collecting my luggage, I found, as I had expected, that the porters had not neglected the glorious opportunity of robbing a woman, and that several articles were missing. Complaints, I knew, would not avail me, and stronger measures seemed hazardous and barely advisable in a lawless out-of-the-way spot, where

> "The simple plan,
> That they should take who have the power,
> And they should keep who can,"

seemed universally practised, and would very likely have been defended by its practitioners upon principle.

It was not so easy to hire a boat as I had been led to ex

pect. The large crowd had made the boatmen somewhat exorbitant in their demands, and there were several reasons why I
should engage one for my own exclusive use, instead of
sharing one with some of my travelling companions. In the
first place, my luggage was somewhat bulky; and, in the
second place, my experience of travel had not failed to teach
me that Americans (even from the Northern States) are
always uncomfortable in the company of coloured people,
and very often show this feeling in stronger ways than by
sour looks and rude words. I think, if I have a little
prejudice against our cousins across the Atlantic—and I
do confess to a little—it is not unreasonable. I have a few
shades of deeper brown upon my skin which shows me
related—and I am proud of the relationship—to those poor
mortals whom you once held enslaved, and whose bodies
America still owns. And having this bond, and knowing
what slavery is; having seen with my eyes and heard
with my ears proof positive enough of its horrors—let
others affect to doubt them if they will—is it surprising
that I should be somewhat impatient of the airs of
superiority which many Americans have endeavoured to
assume over me? Mind, I am not speaking of all. I have
met with some delightful exceptions.

At length I succeeded in hiring a boat for the modest
consideration of ten pounds, to carry me and my fortunes
to Cruces. My boat was far from uncomfortable. Large
and flat-bottomed, with an awning, dirty it must be confessed, beneath which swung a hammock, of which I took
immediate possession. By the way, the Central Americans
should adopt the hammock as their national badge; but for
sheer necessity they would never leave it. The master of

the boat, the padrone, was a fine tall negro, his crew were four common enough specimens of humanity, with a marked disregard of the prejudices of society with respect to clothing. A dirty handkerchief rolled over the head, and a wisp of something, which might have been linen, bound round the loins, formed their attire. Perhaps, however, the thick coating of dirt which covered them kept them warmer than more civilized clothing, besides being indisputably more economical.

The boat was generally propelled by paddles, but when the river was shallow, poles were used to punt us along, as on English rivers ; the black padrone, whose superior position was indicated by the use of decent clothing, standing at the helm, gesticulating wildly, and swearing Spanish oaths with a vehemence that would have put Corporal Trim's comrades in Flanders to the blush. Very much shocked, of course, but finding it perfectly useless to remonstrate with him, I swung myself in my hammock and leisurely watched the river scene.

The river Chagres rolled with considerable force, now between low marshy shores, now narrowing, between steep, thickly wooded banks. It was liable, as are all rivers in hilly districts, to sudden and heavy floods ; and although the padrone, on leaving Gatun, had pledged his soul to land me at Cruces that night, I had not been long afloat before I saw that he would forfeit his worthless pledge ; for the wind rose to a gale, ruffling the river here and there into a little sea ; the rain came down in torrents, while the river rose rapidly, bearing down on its swollen stream trunks of trees, and similar waifs and strays, which it tossed about like a giant in sport, threatening to snag us with its playthings every moment. And when we came to a sheltered reach, and found that the little fleet of boats which had preceded us had laid to there, I came to the conclusion that, stiff, tired, and hungry, I should have to pass a night upon the river Chagres. All I could get to eat was some guavas, which grew wild upon the banks, and then I watched the padrone curl his long body up among my luggage, and listened to the crew, who had rolled together at the bottom of the boat, snore as peacefully as if they slept between fair linen sheets, in the purest of calico night-gear, and the most unexceptionable of nightcaps, until somehow I fell into a troubled, dreamy sleep.

At daybreak we were enabled to pursue our journey, and in a short time reached Gorgona. I was glad enough to go on shore, as you may imagine. Gorgona was a mere temporary town of bamboo and wood houses, hastily erected to serve as a station for the crowd. In the present rainy season, when the river was navigable up to Cruces, the chief part of the population migrated thither, so that Gorgona was almost deserted, and looked indescribably damp, dirty, and dull. With some difficulty I found a bakery and a butcher's shop. The meat was not very tempting, for the Gorgona butchers did not trouble themselves about joints, but cut the flesh into strips about three inches wide, and of various lengths. These were hung upon rails, so that you bought your meat by the yard, and were spared any difficulty in the choice of joint. I cannot say that I was favourably impressed with this novel and simple way of avoiding trouble, but I was far too hungry to be particular, and buying a strip for a quarter of a real, carried it off to Mac to cook.

Late that afternoon, the padrone and his crew landed me, tired, wretched, and out of temper, upon the miserable wharf of Cruces.

———

## CHAPTER III.

MY RECEPTION AT THE INDEPENDENT HOTEL—A CRUCES TABLE D'HÔTE —LIFE IN CRUCES—AMUSEMENTS OF THE CROWDS—A NOVEL FOUR-POST BED.

THE sympathising reader, who very likely has been laughing heartily at my late troubles, can fancy that I was looking forward with no little pleasurable anticipation to reaching my brother's cheerful home at Cruces. After the long night spent on board the wretched boat in my stiff, clayey dress, and the hours of fasting, the warmth and good cheer of the Independent Hotel could not fail to be acceptable. My brother met me on the rickety wharf with the kindest welcome in his face, although he did not attempt to conceal a smile at my forlorn appearance, and giving the necessary instructions about my luggage, led the way at once to his house, which was situated at the upper end of the street. A capital site, he said, when the rest of the town was under water—which agreeable variety occurred twice or thrice a year unexpectedly. On our way, he rather damped my hopes by expressing his fears that he should be unable to provide his sister with the accommodation he could wish. For you see, he said, the crowd from Panama has just come in, meeting your crowd from Navy Bay; and I shouldn't be at all surprised if very many of

them have no better bed than the store floors.   But, despite
this warning, I was miserably unprepared for the reception
that awaited me.   To be sure, I found Cruces as like Gorgona, in its dampness, dirt, and confusion, as it well could
be; but the crowd from the gold-fields of California had
just arrived, having made the journey from Panama on
mules, and the street was filled with motley groups in pic-
turesque variety of attire.   The hotels were also full of
them, while many lounged in the verandahs after their
day's journey.   Rude, coarse gold-diggers, in gay-coloured
shirts, and long, serviceable boots, elbowed, in perfect
equality, keen Yankee speculators, as close shaven, neat,
and clean on the Isthmus of Panama as in the streets of
New York or New Orleans.   The women alone kept aloof
from each other, and well they might; for, while a very
few seemed not ashamed of their sex, it was somewhat
difficult to distinguish the majority from their male companions, save by their bolder and more reckless voice and
manner.   I must say, however, that many of them adopted
male attire for the journey across the Isthmus only, as it
spared them many compliments which their husbands were
often disposed to resent, however flattering they might be
to their choice.

Through all these I pressed on, stiff, cold, and hungry,
to the Independent Hotel, eagerly anticipating the comforts
which awaited me there.   At length we reached it.   But,
rest! warmth! comfort!—miserable delusions!   Picture to
yourself, sympathising reader, a long, low hut, built of
rough, unhewn, unplaned logs, filled up with mud and
split bamboo; a long, sloping roof and a large veranhah,
already full of visitors.   And the interior: a long room,

gaily hung with dirty calico, in stripes of red and white ;
above it another room, in which the guests slept, having
the benefit of sharing in any orgies which might be going
on below them, through the broad chinks between the
rough, irregular planks which formed its floor. At the
further end, a small corner, partitioned roughly off, formed
a bar, and around it were shelves laden with stores for the
travellers, while behind it was a little room used by
my brother as his private apartment; but three female
travellers had hired it for their own especial use for the
night, paying the enormous sum of £10 for so exclusive a
luxury. At the entrance sat a black man, taking toll of
the comers-in, giving them in exchange for coin or gold-
dust (he had a rusty pair of scales to weigh the latter) a
dirty ticket, which guaranteed them supper, a night's lodging, and breakfast. I saw all this very quickly, and turned
round upon my brother in angry despair.

"What am I to do? Why did you ever bring me to
this place? See what a state I am in—cold, hungry, and
wretched. I want to wash, to change my clothes, to eat,
to——"

But poor Edward could only shrug his shoulders and
shake his head, in answer to my indignant remonstrances.
At last he made room for me in a corner of the crowded
bar, set before me some food, and left me to watch the
strange life I had come to; and before long I soon forgot
my troubles in the novelty of my position.

The difference between the passengers to and from
California was very distinguishable. Those bound for the
gold country were to a certain extent fresh from civilization, and had scarcely thrown off its control; whereas the

homeward bound revelled in disgusting excess of licence.
Although many of the women on their way to California
showed clearly enough that the life of licence they sought
would not be altogether unfamiliar to them, they still retained some appearance of decency in their attire and
manner; but in many cases (as I have before said) the
female companions of the successful gold-diggers appeared
in no hurry to resume the dress or obligations of their sex.
Many were clothed as the men were, in flannel shirt and
boots; rode their mules in unfeminine fashion, but with
much ease and courage; and in their conversation successfully rivalled the coarseness of their lords.   I think, on the
whole, that those French lady writers who desire to enjoy
the privileges of man, with the irresponsibility of the other
sex, would have been delighted with the disciples who
were carrying their principles into practice in the streets
of Cruces.

The chief object of all the travellers seemed to be
dinner or supper; I do not know what term they gave it.
Down the entire length of the Independent Hotel ran a table
covered with a green oilskin cloth, and at proper intervals
were placed knives and forks, plates, and cups and saucers
turned down; and when a new-comer received his ticket,
and wished to secure his place for the coming repast, he
would turn his plate, cup, and saucer up; which mode of
reserving seats seemed respected by the rest.   And as the
evening wore on, the shouting and quarrelling at the door-
way in Yankee twang increased momentarily; while some
seated themselves at the table, and hammering upon it with
the handles of their knives, hallooed out to the excited
nigger cooks to make haste with the slapjack.   Amidst all

this confusion, my brother was quietly selling shirts, boots, trousers, etc., to the travellers; while above all the din could be heard the screaming voices of his touters without, drawing attention to the good cheer of the Independent Hotel. Over and over again, while I cowered in my snug corner, wishing to avoid the notice of all, did I wish myself safe back in my pleasant home in Kingston; but it was too late to find out my mistake now.

At last the table was nearly filled with a motley assemblage of men and women, and the slapjack, hot and steaming, was carried in by the black cooks. The hungry diners welcomed its advent with a shout of delight; and yet it did not seem particularly tempting. But beyond all doubt it was a capital *pièce de résistance* for great eaters; and before the dinner was over, I saw ample reasons to induce any hotel-keeper to give it his patronage. In truth, it was a thick substantial pancake of flour, salt, and water— eggs were far too expensive to be used in its composition; and by the time the supply had disappeared, I thought the largest appetites must have been stayed. But it was followed by pork, strips of beef stewed with hard dumplings, hams, great dishes of rice, jugs of molasses and treacle for sauce; the whole being washed down with an abundance of tea and coffee. Chickens and eggs were provided for those who were prepared to pay for these luxuries of Panama life. But, so scarce and expensive were they, that, as I afterwards discovered, those hotel-keepers whose larders were so stocked would hang out a chicken upon their signposts, as a sure attraction for the richer and more reckless diggers; while the touter's cry of " Eggs and chickens here" was a very telling one. Wine and spirits were also

obtainable, but were seldom taken by the Americans, who
are abstemious abroad as well as at home.

After dinner the store soon cleared. Gambling was a
great attraction; but my brother, dreading its consequences
with these hot-brained armed men, allowed none to take
place in his hotel. So some lounged away to the faro and
monte tables, which were doing a busy trade; others
loitered in the verandah, smoking, and looking at the
native women, who sang and danced fandangos before
them. The whole of the dirty, woe-begone place, which
had looked so wretched by the light of day, was brilliantly
illuminated now. Night would bring no rest to Cruces,
while the crowds were there to be fed, cheated, or amused.
Daybreak would find the faro-tables, with their piles of
silver and little heaps of gold-dust, still surrounded by
haggard gamblers; daybreak would gleam sickly upon the
tawdry finery of the poor Spanish singers and dancers,
whose weary night's work would enable them to live upon
the travellers' bounty for the next week or so. These few
hours of gaiety and excitement were to provide the Cruces
people with food and clothing for as many days; and while
their transitory sun shone, I will do them the justice to say
they gathered in their hay busily. In the exciting race
for gold, we need not be surprised at the strange groups
which line the race-course. All that I wondered at was,
that I had not foreseen what I found, or that my rage for
change and novelty had closed my ears against the warning
voices of those who knew somewhat of the high-road to
California; but I was too tired to moralise long, and begged
my brother to find me a bed somewhere. He failed to do
so completely, and in despair I took the matter in my own

hands; and stripping the green oilskin cloth from the rough table—it would not be wanted again until to-morrow's breakfast—pinned up some curtains round the table's legs, and turned in with my little servant beneath it. It was some comfort to know that my brother, his servants, and Mac brought their mattresses, and slept upon it above us. It was a novel bed, and required some slight stretch of the imagination to fancy it a four-poster; but I was too tired to be particular, and slept soundly.

We were up right early on the following morning; and refreshed with my night's sleep, I entered heartily into the preparations for breakfast. That meal over, the homeward-bound passengers took boats *en route* for Gorgona, while those bound for California hired mules for the land journey to Panama. So after awhile all cleared away, and Cruces was left to its unhealthy solitude.

---

## CHAPTER IV.

AN UNWELCOME VISITOR IN CRUCES—THE CHOLERA—SUCCESS OF THE
 YELLOW DOCTRESS—FEARFUL SCENE AT THE MULE-OWNER'S—THE
 BURYING PARTIES—THE CHOLERA ATTACKS ME.

I DO not think I have ever known what it is to despair, or even to despond (if such were my inclination, I have had some opportunities recently), and it was not long before I began to find out the bright side of Cruces life, and enter into schemes for staying there. But it would be a week or so before the advent of another crowd would wake

Cruces to life and activity again; and in the meanwhile, and until I could find a convenient hut for my intended hotel, I remained my brother's guest.

But it was destined that I should not be long in Cruces before my medicinal skill and knowledge were put to the test. Before the passengers for Panama had been many days gone, it was found that they had left one of their number behind them, and that one—the cholera. I believe that the faculty have not yet come to the conclusion that the cholera is contagious, and I am not presumptuous enough to forestal them; but my people have always considered it to be so, and the poor Cruces folks did not hesitate to say that this new and terrible plague had been a fellow-traveller with the Americans from New Orleans or some other of its favoured haunts. I had the first intima·tion of its unwelcome presence in the following abrupt and unpleasant manner :—

A Spaniard, an old and intimate friend of my brother, had supped with him one evening, and upon returning home had been taken ill, and after a short period of intense suffering had died. So sudden and so mysterious a death gave rise to the rumour that he had been poisoned, and suspicion rested for a time, perhaps not unnaturally, upon my brother, in whose company the dead man had last been. Anxious for many reasons—the chief one, perhaps, the position of my brother—I went down to see the corpse. A single glance at the poor fellow showed me the terrible truth. The distressed face, sunken eyes, cramped limbs, and discoloured shrivelled skin were all symptoms which I had been familiar with very recently; and at once I pronounced the cause of death to be cholera. The Cruces people were mightily angry with me for expressing such an opinion; even my brother, although it relieved him of the odium of a great crime, was as annoyed as the rest. But by twelve o'clock that morning one of the Spaniard's friends was attacked similarly, and the very people who had been most angry with me a few hours previously, came to me now eager for advice. There was no doctor in Cruces; the nearest approach to one was a little timid dentist, who was there by accident, and who refused to prescribe for the sufferer, and I was obliged to do my best. Selecting from my medicine chest—I never travel anywhere without it—what I deemed necessary, I went hastily to the patient, and at once adopted the remedies I considered fit. It was a very obstinate case, but by dint of mustard emetics, warm fomentations, mustard plasters on the stomach and the back, and calomel, at first in large then in gradually smaller doses, I succeeded in saving my first cholera patient in Cruces.

For a few days the terrible disease made such slow progress amongst us that we almost hoped it had passed on its way and spared us; but all at once it spread rapidly, and affrighted faces and cries of woe soon showed how fatally the destroyer was at work. And in so great request were my services, that for days and nights together I scarcely knew what it was to enjoy two successive hours' rest.

And here I must pause to set myself right with my kind reader. He or she will not, I hope, think that, in narrating these incidents, I am exalting my poor part in them unduly. I do not deny (it is the only thing indeed that I have to be proud of) that I *am* pleased and gratified

when I look back upon my past life, and see times now
and then, and places here and there, when and where I
have been enabled to benefit my fellow-creatures suffering
from ills my skill could often remedy. Nor do I think
that the kind reader will consider this feeling an unworthy
one. If it be so, and if, in the following pages, the
account of what Providence has given me strength to do
on larger fields of action be considered vain or egotistical,
still I cannot help narrating them, for my share in them
appears to be the one and only claim I have to interest
the public ear. Moreover I shall be sadly disappointed, if
those years of life which may be still in store for me are
not permitted by Providence to be devoted to similar
usefulness. I am not ashamed to confess—for the gratification is, after all, a selfish one—that I love to be of
service to those who need a woman's help. And where-
ever the need arises—on whatever distant shore—I ask no
greater or higher privilege than to minister to it. After
this explanation, I resume more freely the account of my
labours in Cruces.

It was scarcely surprising that the cholera should
spread rapidly, for fear is its powerful auxiliary, and the
Cruces people bowed down before the plague in slavish
despair. The Americans and other foreigners in the place
showed a brave front, but the natives, constitutionally
cowardly, made not the feeblest show of resistance.
Beyond filling the poor church, and making the priests
bring out into the streets figures of tawdry dirty saints,
supposed to possess some miraculous influence which they
never exerted, before which they prostrated themselves,
invoking their aid with passionate prayers and cries, they

did nothing. Very likely the saints would have got the credit of helping them if they had helped themselves; but the poor cowards never stirred a finger to clean out their close, reeking huts, or rid the damp streets of the rotting accumulation of months. I think their chief reliance was on "the yellow woman from Jamaica with the cholera medicine." Nor was this surprising; for the Spanish doctor, who was sent for from Panama, became nervous and frightened at the horrors around him, and the people soon saw that he was not familiar with the terrible disease he was called upon to do battle with, and preferred trusting to one who was.

It must be understood that many of those who could afford to pay for my services did so handsomely, but the great majority of my patients had nothing better to give their doctress than thanks. The best part of my practice lay amongst the American store and hotel keepers, the worst among the native boatmen and muleteers. These latter died by scores, and among them I saw some scenes of horror I would fain forget, if it were possible. One terrible night, passed with some of them, has often haunted me. I will endeavour to narrate it, and should the reader be supposed to think it highly coloured and doubtful, I will only tell him that, terrible as it seems, I saw almost as fearful scenes on the Crimean peninsula among British men, a few thousand miles only from comfort and plenty.

It was late in the evening when the largest mule-owner in Cruces came to me and implored me to accompany him to his kraal, a short distance from the town, where he said some of his men where dying. One in particular, his head muleteer, a very valuable servant, he was most selfishly anxious for, and, on the way thither, promised me a large remuneration if I should succeed in saving him. Our journey was not a long one, but it rained hard, and the fields were flooded, so that it took us some time to reach the long, low hut which he called his home. I would rather not see such another scene as the interior of that hut presented. Its roof scarcely sheltered its wretched inmates from the searching rain; its floor was the damp, rank turf, trodden by the mules' hoofs and the muleteers' feet into thick mud. Around, in dirty hammocks, and on the damp floor, were the inmates of this wretched place, male and female, the strong and the sick together, breathing air that nearly choked me, accustomed as I had grown to live in impure atmosphere; for beneath the same roof the mules, more valuable to their master than his human servants, were stabled, their fore-feet locked, and beside them were heaps of saddles, packs, and harness. The groans of the sufferers and the anxiety and fear of their comrades were so painful to hear and witness, that for a few minutes I felt an almost uncontrollable impulse to run out into the stormy night, and flee from this plague-spot. But the weak feeling vanished, and I set about my duty. The mule-owner was so frightened that he did not hesitate to obey orders, and, by my directions, doors and shutters were thrown open, fires were lighted, and every effort made to ventilate the place; and then, with the aid of the frightened women, I applied myself to my poor patients. Two were beyond my skill. Death alone could give them relief. The others I could help. But no words of mine could induce them to bear their terrible sufferings like men. They screamed and groaned, not like women, for few would have been so craven-hearted, but like children; calling, in the intervals of violent pain, upon Jesu, the Madonna, and all the saints of heaven whom their lives had scandalised. I stayed with them until midnight, and then got away for a little time. But I had not long been quiet, before the mule-master was after me again. The men were worse; would I return with him. The rain was drifting heavily on the thatched roof, as it only does in tropical climates, and I was tired to death; but I could not resist his appeal. He had brought with him a pair of tall, thick boots, in which I was to wade through the flooded fields; and with some difficulty I again reached the kraal. I found the worst cases sinking fast, one of the others had relapsed, while fear had paralysed the efforts of the rest. At last I restored some order; and, with the help of the bravest of the women, fixed up rude screens around the dying men. But no screens could shut out from the others their awful groans and cries for the aid that no mortal power could give them. So the long night passed away; first a deathlike stillness behind one screen, and then a sudden silence behind the other, showing that the fierce battle with death was over, and who had been the victor. And, meanwhile, I sat before the flickering fire, with my last patient in my lap— a poor, little, brown-faced orphan infant, scarce a year old, was dying in my arms, and I was powerless to save it. It may seem strange, but it is a fact, that I thought more of that little child than I did of the men who were struggling for their lives, and prayed very earnestly and solemnly to God to spare it. But it did not please Him to grant my prayer, and towards morning the wee spirit left this sinful world for the home above it had so lately left, and what was mortal of the little infant lay dead in my arms. Then it was that I began to think—how the idea first arose in my mind I can hardly say—that, if it were possible to take this little child and examine it, I should learn more of the terrible disease which was sparing neither young nor old, and should know better how to do battle with it. I was not afraid to use my baby patient thus. I knew its fled spirit would not reproach me, for I had done all I could for it in life—had shed tears over it, and prayed for it.

It was cold grey dawn, and the rain had ceased, when I followed the man who had taken the dead child away to bury it, and bribed him to carry it by an unfrequented path down to the river-side, and accompany me to the thick retired bush on the opposite bank. Having persuaded him thus much, it was not difficult, with the help of silver arguments to convince him that it would be for the general benefit and his own, if I could learn from this poor little thing the secret inner workings of our common foe; and ultimately he stayed by me, and aided me in my first and last *post mortem* examination. It seems a strange deed to accomplish, and I am sure I could not wield the scalpel or the substitute I then used now, but at that time the excitement, had strung my mind up to a high pitch of courage and determination; and perhaps the daily, almost hourly, scenes of death had made me somewhat callous. I need not linger on this scene, nor give the readers the results of my operation; although novel to me, and decidedly useful, they were what every medical man well knows.

We buried the poor little body beneath a piece of luxuriant turf, and stole back into Cruces like guilty things.

But the knowledge I had obtained thus strangely was very valuable to me, and was soon put into practice. But that I dreaded boring my readers, I would fain give them some idea of my treatment of this terrible disease. I have no doubt that at first I made some lamentable blunders, and, may be, lost patients which a little later I could have saved. I know I came across, the other day, some notes of cholera medicines which made me shudder, and I dare say they have been used in their turn and found wanting. The simplest remedies were perhaps the best. Mustard plasters, and emetics, and calomel; the mercury applied externally, where the veins were nearest the surface, were my usual resources. Opium I rather dreaded, as its effect is to incapacitate the system from making any exertion, and it lulls the patient into a sleep which is often the sleep of death. When my patients felt thirsty, I would give them water in which cinnamon had been boiled. One stubborn attack succumbed to an additional dose of ten grains of sugar of lead, mixed in a pint of water, given in doses of a table-spoonful every quarter of an hour. Another patient, a girl, I rubbed over with warm oil, camphor, and spirits of wine. Above all, I never neglected to apply mustard poultices to the stomach, spine, and neck, and particularly to keep my patient warm about the region of the heart. Nor did I relax my care when the disease had passed by, for danger did not cease when the great foe was beaten off. The patient was left prostrate; strengthening medicines had to be given cautiously, for fever, often of the brain, would follow. But, after all, one great conclusion, which my practice in cholera cases enabled me to come to, was the old one, that few constitutions permitted the use of exactly similar remedies, and that the course of treatment which saved one man, would, if persisted in, have very likely killed his brother.

Generally speaking, the cholera showed premonitory symptoms; such as giddiness, sickness, diarrhœa, or sunken eyes and distressed look; but sometimes the substance followed its forecoming shadow so quickly, and the crisis was so rapid, that there was no time to apply any remedies. An American carpenter complained of giddiness and sickness—warning signs—succeeded so quickly by the worst symptoms of cholera, that in less than an hour his face became of an indigo tint, his limbs were doubled up horribly with violent cramps, and he died.

To the convicts—and if there could be grades of wretchedness in Cruces, these poor creatures were the lowest—belonged the terrible task of burying the dead; a duty to which they showed the utmost repugnance. Not unfrequently, at some fancied alarm, they would fling down their burden, until at last it became necessary to employ the soldiers to see that they discharged the task allotted to them. Ordinarily, the victims were buried immediately after death, with such imperfect rites of sepulture as the harassed frightened priests would pay them, and very seldom was time afforded by the authorities to the survivors to pay those last offices to the departed which a Spaniard and a Catholic considers so important. Once I was present at a terrible scene in the house of a New Granada grandee, whose pride and poverty justified many of the old Spanish proverbs levelled at his caste.

It was when the cholera was at its height, and yet he had left—perhaps on important business—his wife and family, and gone to Panama for three days. On the day after his departure, the plague broke out in his house, and my services were required promptly. I found the miserable household in terrible alarm, and yet confining their exertions to praying to a coarse black priest in a black surplice, who, kneeling beside the couch of the Spanish lady, was praying (in his turn) to some favourite saint in Cruces. The sufferer was a beautiful woman, suffering from a violent attack of cholera, with no one to help her, or even to take from her arms the poor little child they had allowed her to retain. In her intervals of comparative freedom from pain, her cries to the Madonna and her husband were heart-rending to hear. I had the greatest difficulty to rout the stupid priest and his as stupid worshippers, and do what I could for the sufferer. It was very little, and before long the unconscious Spaniard was a widower. Soon after, the authorities came for the body. I never saw such passionate anger and despair as were shown by her relatives and servants, old and young, at the intrusion—rage that she, who had been so exalted in life, should go to her grave like the poor, poor clay she was. Orders were given to bar the door against the convict gang who had come to discharge their unpleasant duty, and while all were busy decking out the unconscious corpse in gayest attire, none paid any heed to me bending over the fire with the motherless child, journeying fast to join its dead parent. I had made more than one effort to escape, for I felt more sick and wretched than at any similar scene of woe; but finding exit impossible, I turned my back upon them, and attended to the dying child. Nor did I heed their actions until I heard orders given to admit the burial party, and then I found that they had dressed the corpse in rich white satin, and decked her head with flowers.

The agitation and excitement of this scene had affected me as no previous horror had done, and I could not help fancying that symptoms were showing themselves in me with which I was familiar enough in others. Leav· ing the dying infant to the care of its relatives (when the Spaniard returned he found himself widowed and childless), I hastened to my brother's house. When there, I felt an unpleasant chill come over me, and went to bed at once. Other symptoms followed quickly, and, before nightfall, I knew full well that my turn had come at last, and that the cholera had attacked me, perhaps its greatest foe in Cruces.

## CHAPTER V.

AMERICAN SYMPATHY—I TAKE AN HOTEL IN CRUCES—MY CUSTOMERS —LOLA MONTES—MISS HAYES AND THE BISHOP—GAMBLING IN CRUCES—QUARRELS AMONGST THE TRAVELLERS—NEW GRANADA MILITARY—THE THIEVES OF CRUCES—A NARROW ESCAPE.

WHEN it became known that their "yellow doctress" had the cholera, I must do the people of Cruces the justice to say that they gave her plenty of sympathy, and would have shown their regard for her more actively, had there been any occasion. Indeed, when I most wanted quiet, it was difficult to keep out the sympathising Americans and sorrowing natives who came to inquire after me; and who, not content with making their inquiries, and leaving their offerings of blankets, flannel, etc., must see with their own eyes what chance the yellow woman had of recovery. The rickety door of my little room could never be kept shut for many minutes together. A visitor would open it silently, poke his long face in with an expression of sympathy that almost made me laugh in spite of my pain, draw it out again, between the narrowest possible opening, as if he were anxious to admit as little air as he could; while another would come in bodily, and after looking at me curiously and inquisitively, as he would eye a horse or nigger he had some thoughts of making a bid for, would help to carpet my room, with the result perhaps of his meditations, and saying, gravely, "Air you better, Aunty Seacole, now? Isn't there a something we can du for you, ma'am?" would as gravely give place to another and another yet, until I was almost inclined to throw something at them, or call them bad names, like the Scotch king does the ghosts in the play.* But, fortunately, the attack was a very mild one, and by the next day all danger had gone by, although I still felt weak and exhausted.

After a few weeks, the first force of the cholera was spent, and although it lingered with us, as though loath to leave so fine a renting-place, for some months, it no longer gave us much alarm; and before long, life went on as briskly and selfishly as ever with the Cruces survivors, and the terrible past was conveniently forgotten. Perhaps it is so everywhere; but the haste with which the Cruces people buried their memory seemed indecent. Old houses found new masters; the mules new drivers; the great Spaniard chose another pretty woman, and had a grand, poor, dirty wedding, and was married by the same lazy black priest who had buried his wife, dead a few months

---

* Mrs. Seacole very likely refers to Macbeth. But it was the witches he abused.—Ed.

back; and very likely they would all have hastened as
quickly to forget their doctress, had circumstances permitted them : but every now and then one of them sickened
and died of the old complaint; and the reputation I had
established founded for me a considerable practice. The
Americans in the place gladly retained me as their medical
attendant, and in one way or other gave me plenty to do;
but, in addition to this, I determined to follow my original
scheme of keeping an hotel in Cruces.

Right opposite my brother's Independent Hotel there
was a place to let which it was considered I could adapt to
my purpose. It was a mere tumble-down hut, with wat-
tled sides, and a rotten thatched roof, containing two rooms,
one small enough to serve as a bedroom. For this charm-
ing residence—very openly situated, and well ventilated—
twenty pounds a month was considered a fair and by no
means exorbitant rent. And yet I was glad to take possession of it; and in a few days had hung its rude walls with
calico of gayest colour in stripes, with an exuberance of
fringes, frills, and bows (the Americans love show dearly),
and prepared it to accommodate fifty dinner guests. I had
determined that it should be simply a *table d'hôte*, and that
I would receive no lodgers. Once, and once only, I relaxed
this rule in favour of two American women, who sent me to
sleep by a lengthy quarrel of words, woke me in the night
to witness its crisis in a fisticuff *duello*, and left in the morning, after having taken a fancy to some of my moveables
which were most easily removeable. I had on my staff my
black servant Mac, the little girl I have before alluded to, and
a native cook. I had had many opportunities of seeing how
my brother conducted his business; and adopted his tariff

of charges. For an ordinary dinner my charge was four shillings; eggs and chickens were, as I have before said, distinct luxuries, and fetched high prices.

Four crowds generally passed through Cruces every' month. In these were to be found passengers to and from Chili, Peru, and Lima, as well as California and America. The distance from Cruces to Panama was not great—only twenty miles, in fact; but the journey, from the want of roads and the roughness of the country, was a most fatiguing one. In some parts—as I found when I made the journey, in company with my brother—it was almost impassable; and for more than half the distance, three miles an hour was considered splendid progress. The great majority of the travellers were rough, rude men, of dirty, quarrelsome habits; the others were more civilized and more dangerous. And it was not long before I grew very tired of life in Cruces, although I made money rapidly, and pressed my brother to return to Kingston. Poor fellow! it would have been well for him had he done so; for he stayed only to find a grave on the Isthmus of Panama.

The company at my *table d'hôte* was not over select; and it was often very difficult for an unprotected female to manage them, although I always did my best to put them in good humour. Among other comforts, I used to hire a black barber, for the rather large consideration of two pounds, to shave my male guests. You can scarcely conceive the pleasure and comfort an American feels in a clean chin; and I believe my barber attracted considerable custom to the British Hotel at Cruces. I had a little outhouse erected for his especial convenience; and there, well provided with towels, and armed with plenty of razors, a

brush of extraordinary size, and a foaming sea of lather,
José shaved the new-comers.  The rivalry to get within
reach of his huge brush was very great; and the threats
used by the neglected, when the grinning black was considered guilty of any interested partiality, were of the
fiercest description.

This duty over, they and their coarser female companions—many of them well known to us, for they travelled backwards and forwards across the Isthmus, hanging
on to the foolish gold-finders—attacked the dinner, very
often with great lack of decency.  It was no use giving
them carving-knives and forks, for very often they laid
their own down to insert a dirty hairy hand into a full
dish; while the floor soon bore evidences of the great
national American habit of expectoration.  Very often
quarrels would arise during the progress of dinner; and
more than once I thought the knives, which they nearly
swallowed at every mouthful, would have been turned
against one another.  It was, I always thought, extremely
fortunate that the reckless men rarely stimulated their
excitable passions with strong drink.  Tea and coffee were
the common beverages of the Americans; Englishmen, and
men of other nations, being generally distinguishable by
their demand for wine and spirits.  But the Yankee's
capacity for swilling tea and coffee was prodigious.  I saw
one man drink ten cups of coffee; and finding his appetite
still unsatisfied, I ran across to my brother for advice.
There was a merry twinkle in his eyes as he whispered,
"I always put in a good spoonful of salt after the sixth
cup.  It chokes them off admirably."

It was no easy thing to avoid being robbed and cheated by the less scrupulous travellers; although I think it was only the 'cutest Yankee who stood any fair chance of out-witting me. I remember an instance of the biter bit, which I will narrate, hoping it may make my reader laugh as heartily as its recollection makes me. He was a tall, thin Yankee, with a furtive glance of the eyes, and an amazing appetite, which he seemed nothing loath to indulge : his appetite for eggs especially seemed unbounded. Now, I have more than once said how expensive eggs were; and this day they happened to be eightpence apiece. Our plan was to charge every diner according to the number of shells found upon his plate. Now, I noticed how eagerly my thin guest attacked my eggs, and marvelled somewhat at the scanty pile of shells before him. My suspicions once excited, I soon fathomed my Yankee friend's dodge. As soon as he had devoured the eggs, he conveyed furtively the shells beneath the table, and distributed them impartially at the feet of his companions. I gave my little black maid a piece of chalk, and instructions ; and creeping under the table, she counted the scattered shells, and chalked the number on the tail of his coat. And when he came up to pay his score, he gave up his number of eggs in a loud voice; and when I contradicted him, and referred to the coat-*tale* in corroboration of *my* score, there was a general laugh against him. But there was a nasty expression in his cat-like eyes, and an unpleasant allusion to mine, which were not agreeable, and dissuaded me from playing any more practical jokes upon the Yankees.

I followed my brother's example closely, and forbade

all gambling in my hotel. But I got some idea of its fruits from the cases brought to me for surgical treatment from the faro and monte tables. Gambling at Cruces, and on the Isthmus generally, was a business by which money was wormed out of the gold-seekers and gold-finders. No attempt was made to render it attractive, as I have seen done elsewhere. The gambling-house was often plainer than our hotels; and but for the green tables, with their piles of money and gold-dust, watched over by a well-armed determined banker, and the eager gamblers around, you would not know that you were in the vicinity of a spot which the English at home designate by a very decided and extreme name. A Dr. Casey—everybody familiar with the Americans knows their fondness for titles—owned the most favoured·table in Cruces ; and this, although he was known to be a reckless and unscrupulous villain. Most of them knew that he had been hunted out of San Francisco ; and at that time—years before the Vigilance Committee commenced their labours of purification—a man too bad for that city must have been a prodigy of crime : and yet, and although he was violent-tempered, and had a knack of referring the slightest dispute to his revolver; his table was always crowded; probably because—the greatest rogues have some good qualities—he was honest in his way, and played fairly.

Occasionally some distinguished passengers passed on the upward and downward tides of rascality and ruffianism, that swept periodically through Cruces. Came one day, Lola Montes, in the full zenith of her evil fame, bound for California, with a strange suite. A good-looking, bold woman, with fine, bad eyes, and a determined bearing;

dressed ostentatiously in perfect male attire, with shirt-collar turned down over a velvet lapelled coat, richly worked shirt-front, black hat, French unmentionables, and natty, polished boots with spurs. She carried in her hand a handsome riding-whip, which she could use as well in the streets of Cruces as in the towns of Europe; for an impertinent American, presuming—perhaps not unnaturally—upon her reputation, laid hold jestingly of the tails of her long coat, and as a lesson received a cut across his face that must have marked him for some days. I did not wait to see the row that followed, and was glad when the wretched woman rode off on the following morning. A very different notoriety followed her at some interval of time—Miss Catherine Hayes, on her successful singing tour, who disappointed us all by refusing to sing at Cruces; and after her came an English bishop from Australia, who need have been a member of the church militant to secure his pretty wife from the host of admirers she had gained during her day's journey from Panama.

Very quarrelsome were the majority of the crowds, holding life cheap, as all bad men strangely do—equally prepared to take or lose it upon the slightest provocation. Few tales of horror in Panama could be questioned on the ground of improbability. Not less partial were many of the natives of Cruces to the use of the knife; preferring, by the way, to administer sly stabs in the back, when no one was by to see the dastard blow dealt. Terribly bullied by the Americans were the boatmen and muleteers, who were reviled, shot, and stabbed by these free and independent filibusters, who would fain whop all creation abroad as they do their slaves at home. Whenever any Englishmen were present, and in a position to interfere with success, this bullying was checked; and they found, instead of the poor Spanish Indians, foemen worthy of their steel or lead. must do them credit to say, that they were never loath to fight any one that desired that passing excitement, and thought little of ending their journey of life abruptly at the wretched wayside town of Cruces. It very often happened so, and over many a hasty head and ready hand have I seen the sod roughly pressed down, their hot hearts stilled suddenly in some senseless quarrel. And so in time I grew to have some considerable experience in the treatment of knife and gun-shot wounds.

One night I heard a great noise outside my window, and on rising found a poor boatman moaning piteously, and in a strange jumble of many languages begging me to help him. At first I was afraid to open the door, on account of the noisy mob which soon joined him, for villainy was very shrewd at Cruces; but at last I admitted him, and found that the poor wretch's ears had been cruelly split by some hasty citizen of the United States. I stitched them up as well as I could, and silenced his cries. And at any time, if you happened to be near the river when a crowd were arriving or departing, your ears would be regaled with a choice chorus of threats, of which ear-splitting, eye-gouging, cow-hiding, and the application of revolvers were the mildest. Against the negroes, of whom there were many in the Isthmus, and who almost invariably filled the municipal offices, and took the lead in every way, the Yankees had a strong prejudice; but it was wonderful to see how freedom and equality elevate men, and the same negro who perhaps in Tennessee would have cowered like a beaten child or dog beneath an American's uplifted hand, would face him boldly here, and by equal courage and superior physical strength cow his old oppressor.

When more than ordinary squabbles occurred in the street or at the gambling-tables, the assistance of the soldier-police of New Granada was called in, and the affair sometimes assumed the character of a regular skirmish. The soldiers—I wish I could speak better of them—were a dirty, cowardly, indolent set, more prone to use their knives than their legitimate arms, and bore old rusty muskets, and very often marched unshod. Their officers were in outward appearance a few shades superior to the men they commanded, but, as respects military proficiency, were their equals. Add to this description of their *personnel* the well-known fact, that you might commit the grossest injustice, and could obtain the simplest justice only by lavish bribery, and you may form some idea of our military protectors.

Very practised and skilful in thieving were the native population of Cruces—I speak of the majority, and except the negroes always more inclined to do a dishonest night's labour at great risk, than an honest day's work for fair wages; for justice was always administered strictly to the poor natives—it was only the foreigners who could evade it or purchase exemption. Punishment was severe; and in extreme cases the convicts were sent to Carthagena, there to suffer imprisonment of a terrible character. Indeed, from what I heard of the New Granada prisons, I thought no other country could match them, and continued to think so until I read how the ingenuity in cruelty of his Majesty the King of Naples put the torturers of the New Granada Republic to the blush.

I generally avoided claiming the protection of the law whilst on the Isthmus, for I found it was—as is the case in civilized England from other causes—rather an expensive luxury. Once only I took a thief caught in the act before the alcalde, and claimed the administration of justice. The court-house was a low bamboo shed, before which some dirty Spanish-Indian soldiers were lounging; and inside, the alcalde, a negro, was reclining in a dirty hammock, smoking coolly, hearing evidence, and pronouncing judgment upon the wretched culprits, who were trembling before his dusky majesty. I had attended him while suffering from an attack of cholera, and directly he saw me he rose from his hammock, and received me in a ceremonious, grand manner, and gave orders that coffee should be brought to me. He had a very pretty white wife, who joined us; and then the alcalde politely offered me a *cigarito*—having declined which, he listened to my statement with great attention. All this, however, did not prevent my leaving the necessary fee in furtherance of justice, nor his accepting it. Its consequence was, that the thief, instead of being punished as a criminal, was ordered to pay me the value of the stolen goods; which, after weeks of hesitation and delay, she eventually did, in pearls, combs, and other curiosities.

Whenever an American was arrested by the New Granada authorities, justice had a hard struggle for the mastery, and rarely obtained it. Once I was present at the court-house, when an American was brought in heavily ironed, charged with having committed a highway robbery —if I may use the term where there were no roads—on some travellers from Chili. Around the frightened soldiers

swelled an angry crowd of brother Americans, abusing and
threatening the authorities in no measured terms, all of
them indignant that a nigger should presume to judge one
of their countrymen. At last their violence so roused the
sleepy alcalde, that he positively threw himself from his
hammock, laid down his cigarito, and gave such very determined orders to his soldiers that he succeeded in checking
the riot. Then, with an air of decision that puzzled everybody, he addressed the crowd, declaring angrily, that since
the Americans came the country had known no peace, that
robberies and crimes of every sort had increased, and ending
by expressing his determination to make strangers respect
the laws of the Republic, and to retain the prisoner ; and
if found guilty, punish him as he deserved. The Americans
seemed too astonished at the audacity of the black man,
who dared thus to beard them, to offer any resistance ; but I
believe that the prisoner was allowed ultimately to escape.

I once had a narrow escape from the thieves of Cruces.
I had been down to Chagres for some stores, and returning,
late in the evening, too tired to put away my packages,
had retired to rest at once. My little maid, who was not
so fatigued as I was, and slept more lightly, woke me in
the night to listen to a noise in the thatch, at the further
end of the store ; but I was so accustomed to hear the half-
starved mules of Cruces munching my thatch, that I
listened lazily for a few minutes, and then went unsus-
piciously into another heavy sleep. I do not know how
long it was before I was again awoke by the child's loud
screams and cries of " Hombre—landro ;" and sure enough,
by the light of the dying fire, I saw a fellow stealing away
with my dress, in the pocket of which was my purse. I was

about to rush forward, when the fire gleamed on a villainous-looking knife in his hand; so I stood still, and screamed loudly, hoping to arouse my brother over the way. For a moment the thief seemed inclined to silence me, and had taken a few steps forward, when I took up an old rusty horse-pistol which my brother had given me that I might look determined, and snatching down the can of ground coffee, proceeded to prime it, still screaming as loudly as my strong lungs would permit, until the rascal turned tail and stole away through the roof. The thieves usually buried their spoil like dogs, as they were; but this fellow had only time to hide it behind a bush, where it was found on the following morning, and claimed by me.

## CHAPTER VI.

MIGRATION TO GORGONA — FAREWELL DINNERS AND SPEECHES — A BUILDING SPECULATION — LIFE IN GORGONA — SYMPATHY WITH AMERICAN SLAVES — DR. CASEY IN TROUBLE—FLOODS AND FIRES—YANKEE INDEPENDENCE AND FREEDOM.

I REMAINED at Cruces until the rainy months came to an end, and the river grew too shallow to be navigable by the boats higher up than Gorgona; and then we all made preparations for a flitting to that place. But before starting, it appeared to be the custom for the store and hotel keepers to exchange parting visits, and to many of these parties I, in virtue of my recent services to the community, received invitations. The most important social meeting took place on the anniversary of the declaration of American independence, at my brother's hotel, where a score of zealous Americans dined most heartily—as they never fail to do;

and, as it was an especial occasion, drank champagne liberally at twelve shillings a bottle. And, after the usual patriotic toasts had been duly honoured, they proposed "the ladies," with an especial reference to myself, in a speech which I thought worth noting down at the time. The spokesman was a thin, sallow-looking American, with a pompous and yet rapid delivery, and a habit of turning over his words with his quid before delivering them, and clearing his mouth after each sentence, perhaps to make room for the next. I shall beg the reader to consider that the blanks express the time expended on this operation. He dashed into his work at once, rolling up and getting rid of his sentences as he went on :—

"Well, gentlemen, I expect you'll all support me in a drinking of this toast that I du ——. Aunty Seacole, gentlemen; I give you, Aunty Seacole ——. We can't du less for her, after what she's done for us ——, when the cholera was among us, gentlemen ——, not many months ago ——. So, I say, God bless the best yaller woman He ever made ——, from Jamaica, gentlemen ——, from the Isle of Springs—Well, gentlemen, I expect there are only tu things we're vexed for ——; and the first is, that she ain't one of us ——, a citizen of the great United States ——; and the other thing is, gentlemen ——, that Providence made her a yaller woman. I calculate, gentlemen, you're all as vexed as I am that she's not wholly white ——, but I du reckon on your rejoicing with me that she's so many shades removed from being entirely black ——; and I guess, if we could bleach her by any means we would ——, and thus make her as acceptable in any company as she deserves to be ——. Gentlemen, I give you Aunty Seacole!"

And so the orator sat down amidst much applause. It may be supposed that I did not need much persuasion to return thanks, burning, as I was, to tell them my mind on the subject of my colour. Indeed, if my brother had not checked me, I should have given them my thoughts some-what too freely. As it was, I said :—

" Gentlemen,—I return you my best thanks for your kindness in drinking my health. As for what I have done in Cruces, Providence evidently made me to be useful, and I can't help it. But, I must say, that I don't alto-gether appreciate your friend's kind wishes with respect to my complexion. If it had been as dark as any nigger's, I should have been just as happy and as useful, and as much respected by those whose respect I value ; and as to his offer of bleaching me, I should, even if it were practicable, decline it without any thanks. As to the society which the process might gain me admission into, all I can say is, that, judging from the specimens I have met with here and elsewhere, I don't think that I shall lose much by being excluded from it. So, gentlemen, I drink to you and the general reformation of American manners."

I do not think that they altogether admired my speech, but I was a somewhat privileged person, and they laughed at it good-naturedly enough. Perhaps (for I was not in the best humour myself) I should have been better pleased if they had been angry.

Rightly, I ought to have gone down to Gorgona a few weeks before Cruces was deserted, and secured an hotel ; but I did not give up all hope of persuading my brother to leave the Isthmus until the very last moment, and then, of course, a suitable house was not to be hired in Gorgona for love or money. Seeing his fixed determination to stay, I consented to remain with him, for he was young and often ill, and set hard to work to settle myself somewhere. With the aid of an old Jamaica friend, who had settled at Gorgona, I at last found a miserable little hut for sale, and bought it for a hundred dollars. It consisted of one room only, and was, in its then condition, utterly unfit for my purpose; but I determined to set to work and build on to it—by no means the hazardous speculation in Gorgona, where bricks and mortar are unknown, that it is in England. The alcalde's permission to make use of the adjacent ground was obtained for a moderate consideration, and plenty of material was procurable from the opposite bank of the river. An American, whom I had cured of the cholera at Cruces, lent me his boat, and I hired two or three natives to cut down and shape the posts and bamboo poles. Directly these were raised, Mac and my little maid set to work and filled up the spaces between them with split bamboo canes and reeds, and before long my new hotel was ready to be roofed. The building process was simple enough, and I soon found myself in possession of a capital dining-room some thirty feet in length, which was gaily hung with coloured calico, concealing all defects of construction, and lighted with large oil lamps; a store-room, bar, and a small private apartment for ladies. Altogether, although I had to pay my labourers four shillings a day, the whole building did not cost me more than my brother paid for three months' rent of his hotel. I gave the travelling world to understand that I intended to devote my establishment principally to the entertainment of ladies, and the care of those who might fall ill on the route, and I found the scheme answer admirably. And yet, although the speculation paid well, I soon grew as weary of my life in Gorgona as I had been at Cruces; and when I found my brother proof against all persuasion to quit the Isthmus, I began to entertain serious thoughts of leaving him.

Nor was it altogether my old roving inclination which led me to desire a change, although I dare say it had something to do with it. My present life was not agreeable for a woman with the least delicacy or refinement; and of female society I had none. Indeed, the females who crossed my path were about as unpleasant specimens of the fair sex as one could well wish to avoid. With very few exceptions, those who were not bad were very disagreeable, and as the majority came from the Southern States of America, and showed an instinctive repugnance against any one whose countenance claimed for her kindred with their slaves, my position was far from a pleasant one. Not that it ever gave me any annoyance; they were glad of my stores and comforts, I made money out of their wants; nor do I think our bond of connection was ever closer; only this, if any of them came to me sick and suffering (I say this out of simple justice to myself), I forgot everything, except that she was my sister, and that it was my duty to help her.

I may have before said that the citizens of the New Granada Republic had a strong prejudice against all Americans. It is not difficult to assign a cause for this. In the first place, many of the negroes, fugitive from the Southern States, had sought refuge in this and the other States of Central America, where every profession was open to them;

and as they were generally superior men—evinced perhaps by their hatred of their old condition and their successful flight—they soon rose to positions of eminence in New Granada. In the priesthood, in the army, in all municipal offices, the self-liberated negroes were invariably found in the foremost rank; and the people, for some reason—perhaps because they recognised in them superior talents for administration—always respected them more than, and preferred them to, their native rulers. So that, influenced naturally by these freed slaves, who bore themselves before their old masters bravely and like men, the New Granada people were strongly prejudiced against the Americans. And in the second and third places, they feared their quarrelsome, bullying habits—be it remembered that the crowds to California were of the lowest sorts, many of whom have since fertilised Cuban and Nicaraguan soil—and dreaded their schemes for annexation. To such an extent was this amusingly carried, that when the American Railway Company took possession of Navy Bay, and christened it Aspinwall, after the name of their Chairman, the native authorities refused to recognise their right to name any portion of the Republic, and pertinaciously returned all letters directed to Aspinwall, with "no such place known" marked upon them in the very spot for which they were intended. And, in addition to this, the legal authorities refused to compel any defendant to appear who was described as of Aspinwall, and put every plaintiff out of court who described himself as residing in that unrecognised place.

Under these circumstances, my readers can easily understand that when any Americans crossed the Isthmus, accompanied by their slaves, the Cruces and Gorgona people were restlessly anxious to whisper into their ears offers of freedom and hints how easy escape would be. Nor were the authorities at all inclined to aid in the recapture of a runaway slave. So that, as it was necessary for the losers to go on with the crowd, the fugitive invariably escaped. It is one of the maxims of the New Granada constitution—as it is, I believe, of the English—that on a slave touching its soil his chains fall from him. Rather than irritate so dangerous a neighbour as America, this rule was rarely supported; but I remember the following instance of its successful application.

A young American woman, whose character can be best described by the word "vicious," fell ill at Gorgona, and was left behind by her companions under the charge of a young negro, her slave, whom she treated most inhumanly, as was evinced by the poor girl's frequent screams when under the lash. One night her cries were so distressing, that Gorgona could stand it no longer, but broke into the house and found the chattel bound hand and foot, naked, and being severely lashed. Despite the threats and astonishment of the mistress, they were both carried off on the following morning, before the alcalde, himself a man of colour, and of a very humane disposition. When the particulars of the case were laid before him, he became strongly excited, and called upon the woman to offer an explanation of her cruelty. She treated it with the coolest unconcern—"The girl was her property, worth so many dollars, and a child at New Orleans; had misbehaved herself, and been properly corrected. The alcalde must be drunk or a fool, or both together, to interfere between an American and her property." Her coolness vanished, however, when the alcalde turned round to the girl and told her that she was free to leave her mistress when she liked; and when she heard the irrepressible cheering of the crowded court-hut at the alcade's humanity and boldness, and saw the slave's face flush with delight at the judge's words, she became terribly enraged; made use of the most fearful threats, and would have wreaked summary vengeance on her late chattel had not the clumsy soldiery interfered. Then, with demoniac refinement of cruelty, she bethought herself of the girl's baby at New Orleans still in her power, and threatened most horrible torture to the child if its mother dared to accept the alcalde's offer.

The poor girl trembled and covered her face with her hands, as though to shut out some fearful sight, and, I think, had we not persuaded her to the contrary, that she would have sacrificed her newly won freedom for the child's sake. But we knew very well that when the heat of passion had subsided, the threatener would be too 'cute to injure her own property; and at once set afloat a sub-scription for the purchase of the child. The issue of the tale I do not know, as the woman was very properly re-moved into the interior of the country.

Life at Gorgona resembled life at Cruces so nearly that it does not need a separate description. Down with the store and hotel keepers came the muleteers and mules, porters and hangers-on, idlers and thieves, gamblers and dancing women; and soon the monte-tables were fitted up, and plying their deadly trade; and the dancers charmed the susceptible travellers as successfully in the dirty streets of Gorgona as they had previously done in the unwholesome precincts of Cruces. And Dr. Casey was very nearly getting himself into serious trouble, from too great a readiness to use his revolver. Still, he had a better excuse for bloodshed this time than might have been found for his previous breaches of the sixth commandment. Among the desperadoes who frequented his gambling-hut, during their short stay in Gorgona, was conceived the desperate plan of putting out the lights, and upsetting Casey's table—trusting in the confusion to carry off the piles of money upon it. The first part of their programme was successfully carried out; but the second was frustrated by the Doctor promptly firing his revolver into the dark, and hitting an unoffending boy in the hip. And at this crisis the Gorgona police entered, carried off all the parties they could lay hands upon (including the Doctor) to prison, and brought the wounded boy to me.

On the following morning came a most urgent request that I would visit the imprisoned Doctor. I found him desperately angry, but somewhat nervous too, for the alcalde was known to be no friend to the Americans, owed Casey more than one grudge, and had shown recently a disposition to enforce the laws.

"I say, Mrs. Seacole, how's that —— boy?"

"Oh, Dr. Casey, how could you shoot the poor lad, and now call him bad names, as though he'd injured you? He is very ill indeed—may die; so I advise you to think seriously of your position."

"But, Madame Seacole" (this in a very altered tone), "*you'll* surely help me? *you'll* surely tell the alcalde that the wound's a slight one? He's a friend of yours, and will let me out of this hole. Come, Madame Seacole, you'll never leave me to be murdered by these bloodthirsty savages?"

"What can I do or say, Dr. Casey? I must speak the truth, and the ball is still in the poor lad's hip," I answered, for I enjoyed the fellow's fear too much to help him. However, he sent some of his friends to the boy's father, and bribed him to take the lad from my care, and send him to Navy Bay, to a surgeon there. Of course, he never returned to prosecute Dr. Casey; and he was left with the alcalde only to deal with, who, although he hated the man, could not resist his money, and so set him free.

Gorgona, lying lower than Cruces, its inhabitants more frequently enjoyed the excitement of a flood. After heavy rains, the river would rise so rapidly that in a few hours the chief part of the place would be under water. On such occasions the scene was unusually exciting. As the water crept up the street, the frightened householders kept removing their goods and furniture to higher ground; while here and there, where the waters had surrounded them unawares, boats were sent to their rescue. The houses, not made to resist much wind or water, often gave way, and were carried down the Chagres. Meanwhile, the thieves were the busiest—the honest folks, forgetting the true old adage, "God helps those who help themselves," confining their exertions to bringing down their favourite saints to the water's edge, and invoking their interposition.

Fortunately my hotel was at the upper end of the town, where the floods had been rarely known to extend; and although there was a sufficient chance of the water reaching me to compel me to have all my stores, etc., ready packed for removal, I escaped. Some distressing losses

occurred. A Frenchman, a near neighbour, whose house
was surrounded by the waters before he could remove his
goods, grew so frantic at the loss, that he obstinately refused to quit his falling house; and some force had to be
used before they could save his life.

Scarcely had the ravages of the last flood been repaired
when fire marked Gorgona for its prey. The conflagration
began at a store by the river-side; but it spread rapidly,
and before long all Gorgona was in danger. The town
happened to be very full that night, two crowds having
met there, and there was great confusion; but at last the
lazy soldier-police, aided by the Americans, succeeded in
pulling down some old crazy huts, and checking the fire's
progress. The travellers were in sore plight, many of
them being reduced to sleep upon their luggage, piled in
the drenched streets. My hotel had some interesting inmates, for a poor young creature, borne in from one of the
burning houses, became a mother during the night; and
a stout little lassie opened its eyes upon this waesome
world during the excitement and danger of a Gorgona
conflagration.

Shortly after this, tired to death of life in Panama, I
handed over my hotel to my brother, and returned to
Kingston. On the way thither I experienced another instance of American politeness, which I cannot help record-
ing; first reminding my readers of what I have previously
said of the character of the Californian travellers. Anxious
to get home quickly, I took my passage in the first steamer
that left Navy Bay—an American one; and late in the evening said farewell to the friends I had been staying with, and
went on board. A very kind friend, an American merchant,

doing a large business at Navy Bay, had tried hard to persuade me to delay my journey until the English company's steamer called; without, however, giving any good reasons for his wish. So, with Mac and my little maid, I passed through the crowd of female passengers on deck, and sought the privacy of the saloon. Before I had been long there, two ladies came to me, and in their cool, straightforward manner, questioned me.

"Where air you going?"

"To Kingston."

"And how air you going?"

"By sea."

"Don't be impertinent, yaller woman. By what conveyance air you going?"

"By this steamer, of course. I've paid for my passage."

They went away with this information; and in a short time eight or nine others came and surrounded me, asking the same questions. My answers—and I was very particular—raised quite a storm of uncomplimentary remarks.

"Guess a nigger woman don't go along with us in this saloon," said one. "I never travelled with a nigger yet, and I expect I shan't begin now," said another; while some children had taken my little servant Mary in hand, and were practising on her the politenesses which their parents were favouring me with—only, as is the wont of children, they were crueller. I cannot help it if I shock my readers; but the *truth* is, that one positively spat in poor little Mary's frightened yellow face.

At last an old American lady came to where I sat, and gave me some staid advice. "Well, now, I tell you for your good, you'd better quit this, and not drive my people

to extremities.  If you do, you'll be sorry for it, I expect."
Thus harassed, I appealed to the stewardess—a tall sour-
looking woman, flat and thin as a dressed-up broomstick.
She asked me sundry questions as to how and when I had
taken my passage; until, tired beyond all endurance, I
said, "My good woman, put me anywhere—under a boat—
in your store-room, so that I can get to Kingston somehow."
But the stewardess was not to be moved.

"There's nowhere but the saloon, and you can't expect
to stay with the white people, that's clear.  Flesh and
blood can stand a good deal of aggravation; but not that.
If the Britishers is so took up with coloured people, that's
their business; but it won't do here."

This last remark was in answer to an Englishman,
whose advice to me was not to leave my seat for any of
them.  He made matters worse; until at last I lost my
temper, and calling Mac, bade him get my things together,
and went up to the captain—a good honest man.  He and
some of the black crew and the black cook, who showed
his teeth most viciously, were much annoyed.  Muttering
about its being a custom of the country, the captain gave
me an order upon the agent for the money I had paid;
and so, at twelve o'clock at night, I was landed again upon
the wharf of Navy Bay.

My American friends were vastly annoyed, but not
much surprised; and two days later, the English steamer,
the "Eagle," in charge of my old friend, Captain B——,
touched at Navy Bay, and carried me to Kingston.

# CHAPTER VII.

THE YELLOW FEVER IN JAMAICA—MY EXPERIENCE OF DEATH-BED
SCENES—I LEAVE AGAIN FOR NAVY BAY, AND OPEN A STORE THERE—
I AM ATTACKED WITH THE GOLD FEVER, AND START FOR ESCRI-
BANOS—LIFE IN THE INTERIOR OF THE REPUBLIC OF NEW GRA-
NADA—A REVOLUTIONARY CONSPIRACY ON A SMALL SCALE—THE
DINNER DELICACIES OF ESCRIBANOS—JOURNEY UP THE PALMILLA
RIVER—A FEW WORDS ON THE PRESENT ASPECT OF AFFAIRS ON
THE ISTHMUS OF PANAMA.

I STAYED in Jamaica eight months out of the year 1853,
still remembered in the island for its suffering and gloom.
I returned just in time to find my services, with many
others, needful; for the yellow fever never made a more
determined effort to exterminate the English in Jamaica
than it did in that dreadful year. So violent was the epidemic, that some of my people fell victims to its fury, a
thing rarely heard of before. My house was full of sufferers—officers, their wives and children. Very often they
were borne in from the ships in the harbour—sometimes
in a dying state, sometimes—after long and distressing
struggles with the grim foe—to recover. Habituated as I
had become with death in its most harrowing forms, I
found these scenes more difficult to bear than any I had
previously borne a part in; and for this reason perhaps,
that I had not only to cheer the death-bed of the sufferer,
but, far more trying task, to soothe the passionate grief of
wife or husband left behind. It was a terrible thing to
see young people in the youth and bloom of life suddenly

stricken down, not in battle with an enemy that threatened their country, but in vain contest with a climate that refused to adopt them. Indeed, the mother country pays a dear price for the possession of her colonies.

I think all who are familiar with the West Indies will acknowledge that Nature has been favourable to strangers in a few respects, and that one of these has been in instilling into the hearts of the Creoles an affection for English people and an anxiety for their welfare, which shows itself warmest when they are sick and suffering. I can safely appeal on this point to any one who is acquainted with life in Jamaica. Another benefit has been conferred upon them by inclining the Creoles to practise the healing art, and inducing them to seek out the simple remedies which are available for the terrible diseases by which foreigners are attacked, and which are found growing under the same circumstances which produce the ills they minister to. So true is it that beside the nettle ever grows the cure for its sting.

I do not willingly care to dwell upon scenes of suffering and death, but it is with such scenes that my life's experience has made me most familiar, and it is impossible to avoid their description now and then; and here I would fain record, in humble spirit, my conclusions, drawn from the bearing of those whom I have now and then accompanied a little distance on their way into the Valley of the Shadow of Death, on the awful and important question of religious feeling. Death is always terrible—no one need be ashamed to fear it. How we bear it depends much upon our constitutions. I have seen some brave men, who have smiled at the cruellest amputation, die trembling like children; while others, whose lives have been spent in avoidance of the least danger or trouble, have drawn their last painful breath like heroes, striking at their foe to the last, robbing him of his victory, and making their defeat a triumph. But I cannot trace *all* the peace and resignation which I have witnessed on many death-beds to temperament alone, although I believe it has much more to do with them than many teachers will allow. I have stood by receiving the last blessings of Christians; and closing the eyes of those who had nothing to trust to but the mercy of a God who will be far more merciful to us than we are to one another; and I say decidedly that the Christian's death is the glorious one, as is his life. You can never find a good man who is not a worker; he is no laggard in the race of life. Three, two, or one score years of life have been to him a season of labour in his appointed sphere; and as the work of the hands earns for us sweet rest by night, so does the heart's labour of a lifetime make the repose of heaven acceptable. This is my experience; and I remember one death, of a man whom I grew to love in a few short weeks, the thought of which stirs my heart now, and has sustained me in seasons of great danger; for before that time, if I had never feared death, I had not learnt to meet him with a brave, smiling face, and this he taught me.

I must not tell you his name, for his friends live yet, and have been kind to me in many ways. One of them we shall meet on Crimean soil. He was a young surgeon, and as busy, light-hearted, and joyous as a good man should be; and when he fell ill they brought him to my house, where I nursed him, and grew fond of him—almost as fond as the poor lady his mother in England far away.

For some time we thought him safe, but at last the most terrible symptoms of the cruel disease showed themselves, and he knew that he must die. His thoughts were never for himself, but for those he had to leave behind; all his pity was for them. It was trying to see his poor hands tremblingly penning the last few words of leave-taking—trying to see how piteously the poor worn heart longed to see once more the old familiar faces of the loved ones in unconscious happiness at home; and yet I had to support him while this sad task was effected, and to give him all the help I could. I think he had some fondness for me, or, perhaps, his kind heart feigned a feeling that he saw would give me joy; for I used to call him "My son—my dear child," and to weep over him in a very weak and silly manner perhaps.

He sent for an old friend, Captain S——; and when he came, I had to listen to the dictation of his simple will—his dog to one friend, his ring to another, his books to a third, his love and kind wishes to all; and that over, my poor son prepared himself to die—a child in all save a man's calm courage. He beckoned me to raise him in the bed, and, as I passed my arms around him, he saw the tears I could not repress, rolling down my brown cheeks, and thanked me with a few words. "Let me lay my head upon your breast;" and so he rested, now and then speaking lowly to himself, "It's only that I miss my mother; but Heaven's will be done." He repeated this many times, until the Heaven he obeyed sent him in its mercy forgetfulness, and his thoughts no longer wandered to his earthly home. I heard glad words feebly uttered as I bent over him—words about "Heaven—

rest—rest"—a holy Name many times repeated; and then with a smile and a stronger voice, "Home! home!" And so in a little while my arms no longer held him.

I have a little gold brooch with his hair in it now. I wonder what inducement could be strong enough to cause me to part with that memorial, sent me by his mother some months later, with the following letter:—

"MY DEAR MADAM,—Will you do me the favour to accept the enclosed trifle, in remembrance of that dear son whose last moments were soothed by your kindness, and as a mark of the gratitude of, my dear Madam,
        "Your ever sincere and obliged,
                "M—— S——."

After this, I was sent for by the medical authorities to provide nurses for the sick at Up-Park Camp, about a mile from Kingston; and leaving some nurses and my sister at home, I went there and did my best; but it was little we could do to mitigate the severity of the epidemic.

About eight months after my return to Jamaica, it became necessary that some one should go to the Isthmus of Panama to wind up the affairs of my late hotel; and having another fit of restlessness, I prepared to return there myself. I found Navy Bay but little altered. It was evening when I arrived there; and my friend Mr. H——, who came to meet me on the wharf, carefully piloted me through the wretched streets, giving me especial warning not to stumble over what looked like three long boxes, loosely covered with the *débris* of a fallen house. They had such a peculiar look about them that I stopped to ask what they were, receiving an answer which revived all my former memories of Darien life, "Oh, they're only three Irishmen killed in a row a week ago, whom its nobody's business to bury."

I went to Gorgona, wound up the affairs of the hotel, and, before returning to Navy Bay, took the occasion of accompanying my brother to the town of Panama. We did not go with the crowd, but rode alone on mules, taking with us three native guides on foot; and although the distance was not much over twenty miles, and we started at daybreak, we did not reach Panama until nightfall. But far from being surprised at this, my chief wonder was that we ever succeeded in getting over the journey. Through sand and mud, over hill and plain—through thick forests, deep gulleys, and over rapid streams, ran the track; the road sometimes being made of logs of wood laid transversely, with faggots stuffed between; while here and there we had to work our way through a tangled network of brushwood, and over broken rocks that seemed to have been piled together as stones for some giant's sling. We found Panama an old-fashioned, irregular town, with queer stone houses, almost all of which had been turned by the traders into stores.

On my return to Navy Bay—or Colon, as the New Granadans would have it called—I again opened a store, and stayed there for three months or so. I did not find that society had improved much in my absence; indeed, it appeared to have grown more lawless. Endless quarrels, often resulting in bloodshed, took place between the strangers and the natives, and disturbed the peace of the town. Once the Spanish were incensed to such an extent, that they planned a general rising against the foreigners;

and but for the opportune arrival of an English war-steamer, the consequences might have been terrible. The Americans were well armed and ready; but the native population far outnumbered them.

Altogether, I was not sorry when an opportunity offered itself to do something at one of the stations of the New Granada Gold-mining Company, Escribanos, about seventy miles from Navy Bay. I made the journey there in a little vessel, all communication by land from Navy Bay being impossible, on account of the thick, dense forests, that would have resisted the attempts of an army to cut its way through them. As I was at this place for some months altogether, and as it was the only portion of my life devoted to gold-seeking, I shall make no apologies for endeavouring to describe the out-of-the-way village-life of New Granada.

Escribanos is in the province of Veraguas, in the State of New Granada—information uninteresting enough, I have little doubt, to all but a very few of my readers. It lies near the mouth of a rivulet bearing that name, which, leaving the river Belen, runs away to the sea on its own account, about a mile from the mouth of that river. It is a great neighbourhood for gold-mines; and about that time companies and private individuals were trying hard to turn them to good account. Near it is the Fort Bowen mine, and several others; some yielding silver, others gold ore, in small quantities. Others lie in the vicinity of the Palmilla—another river, which discharges itself into the sea about ten miles from Escribanos; and there were more eastward of it, near a similar river, the Coquelet. Legends were rife at that time, and they may be revived at no distant date, of the treasures to be found at Cucuyo, Zapetero,

F

Pananomé, and many other Indian villages on their banks, which in times gone by had yielded up golden treasures to the Old World. But at this time the yield of gold did not repay the labour and capital necessary to extract it from the quartz; and it can only prove successful if more economical methods can be discovered than those now used for that purpose.

Carlos Alexander, the alcalde of Escribanos, had made a good thing out of the gold mania. The mine had belonged to him; had been sold at a fine price, and, passing through several hands, had at last come into possession of the Company who were now working it; its former owner settling down as ruler over the little community of two hundred souls that had collected at Escribanos. He was a black man; was fond of talking of his early life in slavery, and how he had escaped; and possessed no ordinary intellect. He possessed, also, a house, which in England a well-bred hound would not have accepted as a kennel; a white wife, and a pretty daughter, with a whity-brown complexion and a pleasant name—Juliana.

Of this mine Mr. Day—by whose invitation, when I saw him at Navy Bay, I went there—was at that time superintendent. He was a distant connection of my late husband, and treated me with great kindness. Strangely enough, we met again in a far different part of the world, and became more closely connected. But I am anticipating.

The major part of the population of Escribanos, including even the women and children, worked at the mine. The labour was hard and disagreeable. I often used to watch them at their work; and would sometimes wander about by myself, thinking it possible that I might tumble across some gold in my rambles. And I once did come upon some heavy yellow material, that brought my heart into my mouth with that strange thrilling delight which all who have hunted for the precious metal understand so well. I think it was very wrong; but I kept the secret of the place from the alcalde and every one else, and filled some bottles with the precious dust, to carry down to Navy Bay. I did not go for some time; but when I did, one of my first visits was to a gold-buyer; and you can imagine my feelings when he coolly laughed, and told me it was some material (I forget its name) very like gold, but —valueless. The worst part of it was that, in my annoyance and shame, I threw all I had away, and among itsom which I had reason to believe subsequently was genuine.

The landing at Escribanos was very difficult, and when the surf ran high, impossible; and I was once witness to a harrowing scene there. A little boat, manned by three sailors, grounded on a rock not far from shore, at a terrible season, when to reach it from the land was, after many attempts, found impossible. The hapless crew lingered on for two days, suffering cruelly from hunger and thirst, their cries ringing in our ears above the storm's pitiless fury. On the third day, two of them took to the sea, and were drowned; the third was not strong enough to leave the boat, and died in it.

I did not stay long at Escribanos, on my first visit, as the alcalde's guest; but, having made arrangements for a longer sojourn, I went back to Navy Bay, where I laid in a good stock of the stores I should have most use for, and returned to Escribanos in safety. I remained there some months, pleased with the novelty of

the life, and busy with schemes for seeking for—or, as the
gold-diggers call it, prospecting for—other mines.

The foreigners were just as troublesome in this little
out-of-the-way place as they were, and are, in every other
part of Central America; and quarrels were as frequent in
our little community as at Cruces or Navy Bay. Indeed,
Alexander had hard work to maintain peace in his small
kingdom; and although ably seconded by Mr. Day, more
than once American disregard of his sway was almost too
strong for him. Very often the few foreigners would
quarrel among themselves; and once when they came to
blows, and an Irishman was stabbed by an American named
Campfield, the alcalde roused himself to punish the culprit.
The native population were glad enough to have an American in their power; and when I heard Alexander give his
men instructions to shoot the culprit if he resisted, I
started off to his hut, and reached it in time to prevent
bloodshed. He was taken and kept in confinement; and
soft-hearted Juliana and I had enough to do to prevent his
being made a stern example of. But we got him off for a
fine of five hundred dollars.

Again the little community of Escribanos was very near
getting up a revolution against its constituted government
—a very common amusement in Central America. Twelve
sailors, deserters from an American ship, found their way
there, and before long plotted to dethrone Alexander, and
take possession of the mine. Mr. Day gained information
of their plan. The whole population of Escribanos were
roused and warned; and arming a score of the boldest
natives, he surrounded the house in which they were, and
captured the conspirators, who were too much taken by

surprise to offer resistance, and sent them down to Navy
Bay, there to be handed over to the Government whose
service they had left.

Of course, my medical skill did not rust for want of
practice at Escribanos. The place was not healthy, and
strangers to the climate suffered severely. A surgeon himself, sent there by the West Granada Gold-mining Company,
was glad to throw *his* physic to the dogs, and be cured in
my way by mine; while I was fortunately able to nurse
Mr. Day through a sharp attack of illness.

In consequence of the difficulty of communication with
Navy Bay, our fare was of the simplest at Escribanos. It
consisted mainly of salt meat, rice, and roasted Indian corn.
The native fare was not tempting, and some of their delicacies were absolutely disgusting. With what pleasure, for
instance, could one foreign to their tastes and habits dine
off a roasted monkey, whose grilled head bore a strong resemblance to a negro baby's? And yet the Indians used
to bring them to us for sale, strung on a stick. They were
worse still stewed in soup, when it was positively frightful
to dip your ladle in unsuspectingly, and bring up what
closely resembled a brown baby's limb. I got on better
with the parrots, and could agree with the "senorita, buono
buono" with which the natives recommended them; and
yet their flesh, what little there was of it, was very coarse
and hard. Nor did I always refuse to concede praise to a
squirrel, if well cooked. But although the flesh of the
iguana—another favourite dish—was white and tender as
any chicken, I never could stomach it. These iguanas
are immense green lizards, or rather moderate-sized
crocodiles, sometimes three feet in length, but weighing

generally about seven or eight pounds. The Indians used to bring them down in boats, alive, on their backs, with their legs tied behind them; so that they had the most comical look of distress it is possible to imagine. The Spanish Indians have a proverb referring to an iguana so bound, the purport of which has slipped from my memory, but which shows the habit to be an old one. Their eggs are highly prized, and their captors have a cruel habit of extracting these delicacies from them while alive, and roughly sewing up the wound, which I never could muster sufficient courage to witness.

The rivers near Escribanos were well stocked with crocodiles, the sea had its fair share of sharks, while on land you too often met with snakes and other venomous reptiles. The sting of some of them was very dangerous. One man, who was bitten when I was there, swelled to an enormous size, and bled even at the roots of his hair. The remedy of the natives appeared to be copious bleeding.

Before I left Escribanos I made a journey, in company with a gentleman named Little, my maid, and the alcalde's daughter, into the interior of the country, for a short distance, following the course of the Palmilla river. This was for the purpose of prospecting a mine on that river, said to be obtainable at an easy price. Its course was a very winding one; and we often had to leave the canoe and walk through the shallow waters, that every now and then interfered with our progress. As we progressed, Little carefully sounded the channel of the river, with the view of ascertaining to what extent it was navigable.

The tropical scenery was very grand; but I am afraid I only marked what was most curious in it—at least, that is foremost in my memory now. I know I wondered much what motive Nature could have had in twisting the roots and branches of the trees into such strange fantastic contortions. I watched with unfailing interest the birds and animals we disturbed in our progress, from the huge peccary or wild boar, that went tearing through the brushwood, to the tiniest bright-hued bird that dashed like a flash of many-coloured fire before our eyes. And very much surprised was I when the Indians stopped before a large tree, and on their making an incision in the bark with a matcheto (hatchet), there exuded a thick creamy liquid, which they wished me to taste, saying that this was the famous milk-tree. I needed some persuasion at first; but when I had tasted some upon a biscuit, I was so charmed with its flavour that I should soon have taken more than was good for me had not Mr. Little interfered with some judicious advice. We reached the mine, and brought back specimens of the quartz, some of which I have now.

Soon after this I left Escribanos, and stopping but a short time at Navy Bay, came on direct to England. I had claims on a Mining Company which are still unsatisfied; I had to look after my share in the Palmilla Mine speculation; and, above all, I had long been troubled with a secret desire to embark in a very novel speculation, about which I have as yet said nothing to the reader. But before I finally leave the republic of New Granada, I may be allowed to write a few words on the present aspect of affairs on the Isthmus of Panama.

Recent news from America bring the intelligence that the Government of the United States has at length succeeded in finding a reasonable excuse for exercising a pro-

tectorate over, or in other words annexing, the Isthmus of
Panama. To any one at all acquainted with American
policy in Central America, this intelligence can give no
surprise; our only wonder being that some such excuse
was not made years ago. At this crisis, then, a few remarks from the humblest observer of life in the republic
of New Granada must possess some interest for the curious,
if not value.

I found something to admire in the people of New
Granada, but not much; and I found very much more to
condemn most unequivocally. Whatever was of any worth
in their institutions, such as their comparative freedom, religious toleration, etc., was owing mainly to the negroes who
had sought the protection of the republic. I found the
Spanish Indians treacherous, passionate, and indolent, with
no higher aim or object but simply to enjoy the present after
their own torpid, useless fashion. Like most fallen nations,
they are very conservative in their habits and principles;
while the blacks are enterprising, and in their opinions
incline not unnaturally to democracy. But for their old
antipathy, there is no doubt that the negroes would
lean towards America; but they gladly encourage the
prejudice of the New Granadans, and foster it in every
way. Hence the ceaseless quarrels which have disturbed
Chagres and Panama, until it has become necessary for an
American force to garrison those towns. For humanity
and civilization's sake, there can be little doubt as to the
expediency of this step; but I should not be at all surprised to hear that the republic was preparing to make
some show of resistance against its powerful brother; for,
as the reader will have perceived, the New Granadans'

experiences of American manners have not been favourable; and they do not know, as we do, how little real sympathy the Government of the United States has with the extreme class of its citizens who have made themselves so conspicuous in the great high-road to California.

## CHAPTER VIII.

I LONG TO JOIN THE BRITISH ARMY BEFORE SEBASTOPOL—MY WANDER-INGS ABOUT LONDON FOR THAT PURPOSE—HOW I FAIL—ESTA-BLISHMENT OF THE FIRM OF "DAY AND MARTIN"—I EMBARK FOR TURKEY.

BEFORE I left Jamaica for Navy Bay, as narrated in the last chapter, war had been declared against Russia, and we were all anxiously expecting news of a descent upon the Crimea. Now, no sooner had I heard of war somewhere, than I longed to witness it; and when I was told that many of the regiments I had known so well in Jamaica had left England for the scene of action, the desire to join them became stronger than ever. I used to stand for hours in silent thought before an old map of the world, in a little corner of which some one had chalked a red cross, to enable me to distinguish where the Crimea was; and as I traced the route thither, all difficulties would vanish. But when I came to talk over the project with my friends, the best scheme I could devise seemed so wild and improbable, that I was fain to resign my hopes for a time, and so started for Navy Bay.

But all the way to England, from Navy Bay, I was

turning my old wish over and over in my mind; and
when I found myself in London, in the autumn of 1854,
just after the battle of Alma had been fought, and my old
friends were fairly before the walls of Sebastopol, how to
join them there took up far more of my thoughts than that
visionary gold-mining speculation on the river Palmilla,
which seemed so feasible to us in New Granada, but was
considered so wild and unprofitable a speculation in London. And, as time wore on, the inclination to join my
old friends of the 97th, 48th, and other regiments, battling
with worse foes than yellow fever or cholera, took such
exclusive possession of my mind, that I threw over the
gold speculation altogether, and devoted all my energies
to my new scheme.

Heaven knows it was visionary enough! I had no
friends who could help me in such a project—nay, who
would understand why I desired to go, and what I desired to
do when I got there. My funds, although they might, carefully husbanded, carry me over the three thousand miles,
and land me at Balaclava, would not support me there long;
while to persuade the public that an unknown Creole woman
would be useful to their army before Sebastopol was too improbable an achievement to be thought of for an instant.
Circumstances, however, assisted me.

As the winter wore on, came hints from various
quarters of mismanagement, want, and suffering in the
Crimea; and after the battles of Balaclava and Inkermann, and the fearful storm of the 14th of November, the
worst anticipations were realized. Then we knew that
the hospitals were full to suffocation, that scarcity and
exposure were the fate of all in the camp, and that the

brave fellows for whom any of us at home would have
split our last shilling, and shared our last meal, were
dying thousands of miles away from the active sympathy
of their fellow-countrymen. Fast and thick upon the
news of Inkermann, fought by a handful of fasting and
enfeebled men against eight times their number of picked
Russians, brought fresh and animated to the contest, and
while all England was reeling beneath the shock of that
fearful victory, came the sad news that hundreds were
dying whom the Russian shot and sword had spared, and
that the hospitals of Scutari were utterly unable to shelter,
or their inadequate staff to attend to, the ship-loads of sick
and wounded which were sent to them across the stormy
Black Sea.

But directly England knew the worst, she set about
repairing her past neglect. In every household busy
fingers were working for the poor soldier—money flowed
in golden streams wherever need was—and Christian
ladies, mindful of the sublime example, " I was sick, and
ye visited me," hastened to volunteer their services by
those sick-beds which only women know how to soothe
and bless.

Need I be ashamed to confess that I shared in the
general enthusiasm, and longed more than ever to carry my
busy (and the reader will not hesitate to add experienced)
fingers where the sword or bullet had been busiest, and
pestilence most rife. I had seen much of sorrow and
death elsewhere, but they had never daunted me; and if I
could feel happy binding up the wounds of quarrelsome
Americans and treacherous Spaniards, what delight should
I not experience if I could be useful to my own " sons,"

suffering for a cause it was so glorious to fight and bleed for! I never stayed to discuss probabilities, or enter into conjectures as to my chances of reaching the scene of action. I made up my mind that if the army wanted nurses, they would be glad of me, and with all the ardour of my nature, which ever carried me where inclination prompted, I decided that I *would* go to the Crimea; and go I did, as all the world knows.

Of course, had it not been for my old strong-mindedness (which has nothing to do with obstinacy, and is in no way related to it—the best term I can think of to express it being "judicious decisiveness"), I should have given up the scheme a score of times in as many days; so regularly did each successive day give birth to a fresh set of rebuffs and disappointments. I shall make no excuse to my readers for giving them a pretty full history of my struggles to become a Crimean *heroine!*

My first idea (and knowing that I was well fitted for the work, and would be the right woman in the right place, the reader can fancy my audacity) was to apply to the War Office for the post of hospital nurse. Among the diseases which I understood were most prevalent in the Crimea were cholera, diarrhœa, and dysentery, all of them more or less known in tropical climates; and with which, as the reader will remember, my Panama experience had made me tolerably familiar. Now, no one will accuse me of presumption, if I say that I thought (and so it afterwards proved) that my knowledge of these human ills would not only render my services as a nurse more valuable, but would enable me to be of use to the overworked doctors. That others thought so too, I took with me ample

testimony. I cannot resist the temptation of giving my
readers one of the testimonials I had, it seems so eminently
practical and to the point :—

"I became acquainted with Mrs. Seacole through the
instrumentality of T. B. Cowan, Esq., H. B. M. Consul at
Colon, on the Isthmus of Panama, and have had many
opportunities of witnessing her professional zeal and ability
in the treatment of aggravated forms of tropical diseases.

"I am myself personally much indebted for her inde-
fatigable kindness and skill at a time when I am apt to
believe the advice of a practitioner qualified in the North
would have little availed.

"Her peculiar fitness, in a constitutional point of view,
for the duties of a medical attendant, needs no comment.

    (Signed)            "A. G. M.,

                "Late Medical Officer, West Granada
                Gold-mining Company."

So I made long and unwearied application at the War
Office, in blissful ignorance of the labour and time I was
throwing away. I have reason to believe that I considerably interfered with the repose of sundry messengers, and
disturbed, to an alarming degree, the official gravity of some
nice gentlemanly young fellows, who were working out
their salaries in an easy, off-hand way. But my ridiculous
endeavours to gain an interview with the Secretary-at-War
of course failed, and glad at last to oblige a distracted messenger, I transferred my attentions to the Quartermaster-
General's department. Here I saw another gentleman, who
listened to me with a great deal of polite enjoyment, and

—his amusement ended—hinted, had I not better apply to
the Medical Department; and accordingly I attached myself
to their quarters with the same unwearying ardour. But,
of course, I grew tired at last, and then I changed my
plans.

Now, I am not for a single instant going to blame the
authorities who would not listen to the offer of a motherly
yellow woman to go to the Crimea and nurse her "sons"
there, suffering from cholera, diarrhœa, and a host of lesser
ills. In my country, where people know our use, it would
have been different; but here it was natural enough—
although I had references, and other voices spoke for me—
that they should laugh, good-naturedly enough, at my
offer. War, I know, is a serious game, but sometimes
very humble actors are of great use in it, and if the reader,
when he comes in time to peruse the evidence of those
who had to do with the Sebastopol drama, of my share in
it, will turn back to this chapter, he will confess perhaps
that, after all, the impulse which led me to the War Department was not unnatural.

My new scheme was, I candidly confess, worse devised
than the one which had failed. Miss Nightingale had left
England for the Crimea, but other nurses were still to
follow, and my new plan was simply to offer myself to
Mrs. H—— as a recruit. Feeling that I was one of the
very women they most wanted, experienced and fond of
the work, I jumped at once to the conclusion that they
would gladly enrol me in their number. To go to Cox's,
the army agents, who were most obliging to me, and obtain
the Secretary-at-War's private address, did not take long;
and that done, I laid the same pertinacious siege to his

great house in —— Square, as I had previously done to his place of business.

Many a long hour did I wait in his great hall, while scores passed in and out; many of them looking curiously at me. The flunkeys, noble creatures! marvelled exceedingly at the yellow woman whom no excuses could get rid of, nor impertinence dismay, and showed me very clearly that they resented my persisting in remaining there in mute appeal from their sovereign will. At last I gave that up, after a message from Mrs. H. that the full complement of nurses had been secured, and that my offer could not be entertained. Once again I tried, and had an interview this time with one of Miss Nightingale's companions. She gave me the same reply, and I read in her face the fact, that had there been a vacancy, I should not have been chosen to fill it.

As a last resort, I applied to the managers of the Crimean Fund to know whether they would give me a passage to the camp—once there I would trust to something turning up. But this failed also, and one cold evening I stood in the twilight, which was fast deepening into wintry night, and looked back upon the ruins of my last castle in the air. The disappointment seemed a cruel one. I was so conscious of the unselfishness of the motives which induced me to leave England—so certain of the service I could render among the sick soldiery, and yet I found it so difficult to convince others of these facts. Doubts and suspicions arose in my heart for the first and last time, thank Heaven. Was it possible that American prejudices against colour had some root here? Did these ladies shrink from accepting my aid because my blood flowed beneath a somewhat duskier skin than theirs? Tears streamed down my foolish

cheeks, as I stood in the fast thinning streets ; tears of grief
that any should doubt my motives—that Heaven should
deny me the opportunity that I sought. Then I stood
still, and looking upward through and through the dark
clouds that shadowed London, prayed aloud for help. I
dare say that I was a strange sight to the few passers-by,
who hastened homeward through the gloom and mist of that
wintry night. I dare say those who read these pages will
wonder at me as much as they who saw me did ; but you
must all remember that I am one of an impulsive people,
and find it hard to put that restraint upon my feelings
which to you is so easy and natural.

The morrow, however, brought fresh hope. A good
night's rest had served to strengthen my determination.
Let what might happen, to the Crimea I would go. If in
no other way, then would I upon my own responsibility
and at my own cost. There were those there who had known
me in Jamaica, who had been under my care; doctors who
would vouch for my skill and willingness to aid them, and
a general who had more than once helped me, and
would do so still. Why not trust to their welcome and
kindness, and start at once ? If the authorities had allowed
me, I would willingly have given them my services as a
nurse; but as they declined them, should I not open
an hotel for invalids in the Crimea in my own way ? I
had no more idea of what the Crimea was than the home
authorities themselves perhaps, but having once made up
my mind, it was not long before cards were printed and
speeding across the Mediterranean to my friends before
Sebastopol. Here is one of them :—

## "BRITISH HOTEL.

### MRS. MARY SEACOLE

#### (*Late of Kingston, Jamaica*),

Respectfully announces to her former kind friends, and to the
Officers of the Army and Navy generally,

That she has taken her passage in the screw-steamer " Hollander,"
to start from London on the 25th of January, intending on her arrival at Balaclava to establish a mess table and comfortable quarters for
sick and convalescent officers."

This bold programme would reach the Crimea in the
end of January, at a time when any officer would have
considered a stall in an English stable luxurious quarters
compared to those he possessed, and had nearly forgotten
the comforts of a mess-table. It must have read to them
rather like a mockery, and yet, as the reader will see, I
succeeded in redeeming my pledge.

While this new scheme was maturing, I again met Mr.
Day in England. He was bound to Balaclava upon some
shipping business, and we came to the understanding that
(if it were found desirable) we should together open a
store as well as an hotel in the neighbourhood of the camp.
So was originated the well-known firm of Seacole and
Day (I am sorry to say, the camp wits dubbed it Day and
Martin), which, for so many months, did business upon the
now deserted high-road from the then busy harbour of Balaclava to the front of the British army before Sebastopol.

These new arrangements were not allowed to interfere
in any way with the main object of my journey. A great
portion of my limited capital was, with the kind aid of a
medical friend, invested in medicines which I had reason to

believe would be useful; with the remainder I purchased those home comforts which I thought would be most difficult to obtain away from England.

I had scarcely set my foot on board the "Hollander," before I met a friend. The supercargo was the brother of the Mr. S——, whose death in Jamaica the reader will not have forgotten, and he gave me a hearty welcome. I thought the meeting augured well, and when I told him my plans he gave me the most cheering encouragement. I was glad, indeed, of any support, for, beyond all doubt, my project was a hazardous one.

So cheered at the outset, I watched without a pang the shores of England sink behind the smooth sea, and turned my gaze hopefully to the as yet landless horizon, beyond which lay that little peninsula to which the eyes and hearts of all England were so earnestly directed.

So, cheerily! the good ship ploughed its way eastward ho! for Turkey.

---

## CHAPTER IX.

VOYAGE TO CONSTANTINOPLE—MALTA—GIBRALTAR—CONSTANTINOPLE,
AND WHAT I THOUGHT OF IT—VISIT TO SCUTARI HOSPITAL—MISS
NIGHTINGALE.

I AM not going to risk the danger of wearying the reader with a long account of the voyage to Constantinople, already worn threadbare by book-making tourists. It was a very interesting one, and, as I am a good sailor, I had not even the temporary horrors of sea-sickness to mar it. The weather, although cold, was fine, and the sea good-humouredly calm, and I enjoyed the voyage amazingly. And as day by day we drew nearer to the scene of action, my doubts of success grew less and less, until I had a conviction of the rightness of the step I had taken, which would have carried me buoyantly through any difficulties

On the way, of course, I was called up from my berth at an unreasonable hour to gaze upon the Cape of St. Vincent, and expected to feel duly impressed when the long bay where Trafalgar's fight was won came in view, with the white convent walls on the cliffs above bathed in the early sunlight. I never failed to take an almost childish interest in the signals which passed between the "Hollander" and the fleet of vessels whose sails whitened the track to and from the Crimea, trying to puzzle out the language these children of the ocean spoke in their hurried course, and wondering whether any, or what sufficiently important thing *could* happen which would warrant their stopping on their busy way.

We spent a short time at Gibraltar, and you may imagine that I was soon on shore making the best use of the few hours' reprieve granted to the "Hollander's" weary engines. I had an idea that I should do better alone, so I declined all offers of companionship, and selecting a brisk young fellow from the mob of cicerones who offered their services, saw more of the art of fortification in an hour or so than I could understand in as many years. The pleasure was rather fatiguing, and I was not sorry to return to the market-place, where I stood curiously watching its strange and motley population. While so engaged, I heard for the first time an exclamation which became familiar enough to me afterwards.

"Why, bless my soul, old fellow, if this is not our good old Mother Seacole!" I turned round, and saw two officers, whose features, set in a broad frame of Crimean beard, I had some difficulty in recognising. But I soon remembered that they were two of the 48th, who had been often in my house at Kingston. Glad were the kind-hearted fellows, and not a little surprised withal, to meet their old hostess in the market-place of Gibraltar, bound for the scene of action which they had left invalided; and it was not long before we were talking old times over some wine—Spanish, I suppose—but it was very nasty.

"And you are going to the front, old lady—you, of all people in the world?"

"Why not, my sons?—won't they be glad to have me there?"

"By Jove! yes, mother," answered one, an Irishman. "It isn't many women—God bless them!—we've had to spoil us out there. But it's not the place even for you, who know what hardship is? You'll never get a roof to cover you at Balaclava, nor on the road either." So they rattled on, telling me of the difficulties that were in store for me. But they could not shake my resolution.

"Do you think I shall be of any use to you when I get there?"

"Surely."

"Then I'll go, were the place a hundred times worse than you describe it. Can't I rig up a hut with the packing-cases, and sleep, if need be, on straw, like Margery Daw?"

So they laughed, and drank success to me, and to our next meeting; for, although they were going home invalided, the brave fellows' hearts were with their companions, for all the hardships they had passed through.

We stopped at Malta also, where, of course, I landed, and stared about me, and submitted to be robbed by the lazy Maltese with all a traveller's resignation. Here, also, I met friends—some medical officers who had known me in Kingston; and one of them, Dr. F——, lately arrived from Scutari, gave me, when he heard my plans, a letter of introduction to Miss Nightingale, then hard at work, evoking order out of confusion, and bravely resisting the despotism of death, at the hospital of Scutari.

So on, past beautiful islands and shores, until we are steaming against a swift current, and an adverse wind, between two tower-crested promontories of rock, which they tell me stand in Europe and in Asia, and are connected with some pretty tale of love in days long gone by. Ah! travel where a woman may, in the New World, or the Old, she meets this old, old tale everywhere. It is the one bond of sympathy which I have found existing in three quarters of the world alike. So on, until the cable rattles over the windlass, as the good ship's anchor plunges down fathoms deep into the blue waters of the Bosphorus —her voyage ended.

I do not think that Constantinople impressed me so much as I had expected; and I thought its streets would match those of Navy Bay not unfairly. The caiques, also, of which I had ample experience—for I spent six days here, wandering about Pera and Stamboul in the daytime, and returning to the "Hollander" at nightfall—might

be made more safe and commodious for stout ladies, even
if the process interfered a little with their ornament.
Time and trouble combined have left me with a well-
filled-out, portly form—the envy of many an angular
Yankee female—and, more than once, it was in no slight
danger of becoming too intimately acquainted with the
temperature of the Bosphorus. But I will do the Turkish
boatmen the justice to say that they were as politely careful of my safety as their astonishment and regard for the
well-being of their caicques (which they appear to love
as an Arab does his horse, or an Esquimaux his dogs, and
for the same reason perhaps) would admit. Somewhat
surprised, also, seemed the cunning-eyed Greeks, who
throng the streets of Pera, at the unprotected Creole
woman who took Constantinople so coolly (it would re-
quire something more to surprise her); while the grave
English raised their eyebrows wonderingly, and the more
vivacious French shrugged their pliant shoulders into the
strangest contortions. I accepted it all as a compliment to
a stout female tourist, neatly dressed in a red or yellow
dress, a plain shawl of some other colour, and a simple
straw wide-awake, with bright red streamers. I flatter
myself that I woke up sundry sleepy-eyed Turks, who
seemed to think that the great object of life was to avoid
showing surprise at anything; while the Turkish women
gathered around me, and jabbered about me, in the most
flattering manner.

How I ever succeeded in getting Mr. Day's letters from
the Post-office, Constantinople, puzzles me now; but I
did—and I shall ever regard my success as one of the
great triumphs of my life. Their contents were not very

cheering. He gave a very dreary account of Balaclava and of camp life, and almost dissuaded me from continuing my journey; but his last letter ended by giving me instructions as to the purchases I had best make, if I still determined upon making the adventure; so I forgot all the rest, and busied myself in laying in the stores he recommended.

But I found time, before I left the "Hollander," to charter a crazy caicque, to carry me to Scutari, intending to present Dr. F——'s letter to Miss Nightingale.

It was afternoon when the boatmen set me down in safety at the landing-place of Scutari, and I walked up the slight ascent, to the great dull-looking hospital. Thinking of the many noble fellows who had been borne, or had painfully crept along this path, only to die within that dreary building, I felt rather dull; and directly I entered the hospital, and came upon the long wards of sufferers, lying there so quiet and still, a rush of tears came to my eyes, and blotted out the sight for a few minutes. But I soon felt at home, and looked about me with great interest. The men were, many of them, very quiet Some of the convalescent formed themselves into little groups around one who read a newspaper; others had books in their hands, or by their side, where they had fallen when slumber overtook the readers, while hospital orderlies moved to and fro, and now and then the female nurses, in their quiet uniform, passed noiselessly on some mission of kindness.

I was fortunate enough to find an old acquaintance, who accompanied me through the wards, and rendered it unnecessary for me to trouble the busy nurses. This was an old 97th man—a Sergeant T——, whom I had known in

Kingston, and who was slowly recovering from an attack
of dysentery, and making himself of use here until the
doctors should let him go back and have another " shy at
the Rooshians." He is very glad to meet me, and tells me
his history very socially, and takes me to the bedsides of
some comrades, who had also known me at Up-Park Camp.
My poor fellows! how their eyes glisten when they light
upon an old friend's face in these Turkish barracks—put
to so sad a use, three thousand miles from home. Here
is one of them—" hurt in the trenches," says the Sergeant,
with shaven bandaged head, and bright, restless, Irish eyes,
who hallooes out, " Mother Seacole! Mother Seacole!" in
such an excited tone of voice; and when he has shaken
hands a score of times, falls back upon his pillow very wea-
rily. But I sit by his side, and try to cheer him with
talk about the future, when he shall grow well, and see
home, and hear them all thank him for what he has been
helping to do, so that he grows all right in a few minutes;
but, hearing that I am on the way to the front, gets excited
again; for, you see, illness and weakness make these
strong men as children, not least in the patient unmur-
muring resignation with which they suffer. I think my
Irish friend had an indistinct idea of a "muddle" somewhere, which had kept him for weeks on salt meat and biscuit, until it gave him the " scurvy," for he is very anxious
that I should take over plenty of vegetables, of every sort.
" And, oh! mother!"—and it is strange to hear his almost
plaintive tone as he urges this—" take them plenty of
eggs, mother; we never saw eggs over there."

At some slight risk of giving offence, I cannot resist
the temptation of lending a helping hand here and there—

replacing a slipped bandage, or easing a stiff one. But I do not think any one was offended; and one doctor, who had with some surprise and, at first, alarm on his face, watched me replace a bandage, which was giving pain, said, very kindly, when I had finished, " Thank you, ma'am."

One thought never left my mind as I walked through the fearful miles of suffering in that great hospital. If it is so here, what must it not be at the scene of war—on the spot where the poor fellows are stricken down by pestilence or Russian bullets, and days and nights of agony must be passed before a woman's hand can dress their wounds. And I felt happy in the conviction that *I must* be useful three or four days nearer to their pressing wants than this.

It was growing late before I felt tired, or thought of leaving Scutari, and Dr. S——, another Jamaica friend, who had kindly borne me company for the last half-hour, agreed with me that the caicque was not the safest convey-ance by night on the Bosphorus, and recommended me to present my letter to Miss Nightingale, and perhaps a lodging for the night could be found for me. So, still under the Sergeant's patient guidance, we thread our way through passages and corridors, all used as sick-wards, until we reach the corner tower of the building, in which are the nurses' quarters.

I think Mrs. B——, who saw me, felt more sur-prise than she could politely show (I never found women so quick to understand me as the men) when I handed her Dr. F——'s kind letter respecting me, and apologized for troubling Miss Nightingale. There is that in the Doctor's letter (he had been much at Scutari) which prevents my request being refused, and I am asked to wait until Miss

Nightingale, whose every moment is valuable, can see me.
Meanwhile Mrs. B. questions me very kindly, but with
the same look of curiosity and surprise.

What object has Mrs. Seacole in coming out? This is
the purport of her questions. And I say, frankly, to be of
use somewhere; for other considerations I had not, until
necessity forced them upon me. Willingly, had they accepted me, I would have worked for the wounded, in
return for bread and water. I fancy Mrs. B—— thought
that I sought for employment at Scutari, for she said, very
kindly—

"Miss Nightingale has the entire management of our
hospital staff, but I do not think that any vacancy—"

"Excuse me, ma'am," I interrupt her with, "but I
am bound for the front in a few days;" and my questioner
leaves me, more surprised than ever. The room I waited
in was used as a kitchen. Upon the stoves were cans of
soup, broth, and arrow-root, while nurses passed in and out
with noiseless tread and subdued manner. I thought
many of them had that strange expression of the eyes
which those who have gazed long on scenes of woe or
horror seldom lose.

In half an hour's time I am admitted to Miss Nightingale's presence. A slight figure, in the nurses' dress; with
a pale, gentle, and withal firm face, resting lightly in the
palm of one white hand, while the other supports the
elbow—a position which gives to her countenance a keen
inquiring expression, which is rather marked. Standing
thus in repose, and yet keenly observant—the greatest
sign of impatience at any time* a slight, perhaps unwitting

* Subsequently I saw much of Miss Nightingale, at Balaclava.

motion of the firmly planted right foot—was Florence Nightingale—that Englishwoman whose name shall never die, but sound like music on the lips of British men until the hour of doom.

She has read Dr. F——'s letter, which lies on the table by her side, and asks, in her gentle but eminently practical and business-like way, "What do you want, Mrs. Seacole —anything that we can do for you? If it lies in my power, I shall be very happy."

So I tell her of my dread of the night journey by caicque, and the improbability of my finding the "Hollander" in the dark; and, with some diffidence, threw myself upon the hospitality of Scutari, offering to nurse the sick for the night. Now unfortunately, for many reasons, room even for one in Scutari Hospital was at that time no easy matter to find; but at last a bed was discovered to be unoccupied at the hospital washerwomen's quarters.

My experience of washerwomen, all the world over, is the same—that they are kind soft-hearted folks. Possibly the soap suds they almost live in find their way into their hearts and tempers, and soften them. This Scutari washerwoman is no exception to the rule, and welcomes me most heartily. With her, also, are some invalid nurses; and after they have gone to bed, we spend some hours of the night talking over our adventures, and giving one another scraps of our respective biographies. I hadn't long retired to my couch before I wished most heartily that we had continued our chat; for unbidden and most unwelcome companions took the washerwoman's place, and persisted not only in dividing my bed, but my plump person also. Upon my word, I believe the fleas are the only industrious

creatures in all Turkey.   Some of their relatives would
seem to have migrated into Russia; for I found them in
the Crimea equally prosperous and ubiquitous.

In the morning, a breakfast is sent to my mangled remains, and a kind message from Mrs. B——, having
reference to how I spent the night. And, after an interview
with some other medical men, whose acquaintance I had
made in Jamaica, I shake hands with the soft-hearted
washerwoman, up to her shoulders in soap-suds already,
and start for the " Hollander."

<hr />

## CHAPTER X.

" JEW JOHNNY"—I START FOR BALACLAVA—KINDNESS OF MY OLD
    FRIENDS—ON BOARD THE " MEDORA "—MY LIFE ON SHORE—THE
    SICK WHARF.

DURING my stay in Constantinople, I was accustomed
to employ, as a guide, a young Greek Jew, whose name it
is no use my attempting to spell, but whom I called by the
one common name there—" Johnny." Wishing, however,
to distinguish my Johnny from the legion of other Johnnies,
I prefixed the term Jew to his other name, and addressed
him as Jew Johnny. How he had picked up his knowledge I cannot tell, but he could talk a little broken English, besides French, which, had I been qualified to criti-
cise it, I should have found, perhaps, as broken as his
English. He attached himself very closely to me, and
seemed very anxious to share my fortunes; and after he
had pleaded hard, many times, to be taken to the Crimea,

I gave in, and formally hired him. He was the best and faithfullest servant I had in the Crimea, and, so far from regretting having picked up Jew Johnny from the streets of Pera, I should have been very badly off without him.

More letters come from Mr. Day, giving even worse accounts of the state of things at Balaclava; but it is too late for hesitation now. My plans are perfected, my purchases made, and passage secured in the " Albatross "—a transport laden with cattle and commissariat officers for Balaclava. I thought I should never have transported my things from the " Hollander " to the " Albatross." It was a terrible day, and against the strong current and hurricane of wind Turkish and Greek arms seemed of little avail; but at last, after an hour or more of terrible anxiety and fear, the " Albatross's " side was reached, and I clambered on deck, drenched and wretched.

My companions are cheerful, pleasant fellows, and the short, although somewhat hazardous, voyage across the Black Sea is safely made, and one morning we become excited at seeing a dark rock-bound coast, on which they tell us is Balaclava. As we steam on we see, away to the right, clouds of light smoke, which the knowing travellers tell us are not altogether natural, but show that Sebastopol is not yet taken, until the " Albatross " lays-to within sight of where the " Prince," with her ill-fated companions, went down in that fearful November storm, four short months ago, while application is made to the harbour-master for leave to enter the port of Balaclava. It does not appear the simplest favour in the world that we are applying for—licence to escape from the hazards of the Black Sea. But at last it comes, and we slowly wind through a narrow channel, and emerge into a small land-locked basin, so filled with shipping that their masts bend in the breeze like a wintry forest. Whatever might have been the case at one time, there is order in Balaclava Harbour now, and the "Albatross," with the aid of her boats, moves along to her appointed moorings.

Such a busy scene as that small harbour presented could be rarely met with elsewhere. Crowded with shipping, of every size and variety, from the noble English steamer to the smallest long-shore craft, while between them and the shore passed and repassed innumerable boats; men-of-war's boats, trim and stern; merchant-ship's boats, laden to the gunwales; Greek and Maltese boats, carrying their owners everywhere on their missions of sharp dealing and roguery. Coming from the quiet gloomy sea into this little nook of life and bustle the transition is very sudden and startling, and gives one enough to think about without desiring to go on shore this afternoon.

On the following morning, Mr. Day, apprised of my arrival, came on board the "Albatross," and our plans were laid. I must leave the "Albatross," of course, and, until we decide upon our future, I had better take up my quarters on board the "Medora," which is hired by Government, at a great cost, as an ammunition ship. The proposal was not a very agreeable one, but I have no choice left me. Our stores, too, had to be landed at once. Warehouses were unheard of in Balaclava, and we had to stack them upon the shore and protect them as well as we were able.

My first task, directly I had become settled on board the "Medora," was to send word to my friends of my arrival in the Crimea, and solicit their aid. I gave a Greek idler

one pound to carry a letter to the camp of the 97th, while
I sent another to Captain Peel, who was hard at work
battering the defences of Sebastopol about the ears of the
Russians, from the batteries of the Royal Naval Brigade.
I addressed others to many of the medical men who had
known me in other lands; nor did I neglect to send word
to my kind patron, Sir John Campbell, then command-
ing a division: and my old friends answered my letters most kindly. As the various officers came down on
duty or business to Balaclava they did not fail to find me
out, and welcome me to the Crimea, while Captain Peel
and Sir J. Campbell sent the kindest messages; and when
they saw me, promised me every assistance, the General
adding that he is glad to see me where there is so much to
do. Among others, poor H. Vicars, whose kind face· had
so often lighted up my old house in Kingston, came to
take me by the hand in this out-of-the-way corner of the
world. I never felt so sure of the success of any step as I
did of this, before I had been a week in Balaclava. But
I had plenty of difficulties to contend with on every side.

Among the first, one of the ships, in which were many of
our stores, the "Nonpareil," was ordered out of the harbour
before we could land them all, and there was more than a
probability that she would carry back to Constantinople
many of the things we had most pressing occasion for.
It became necessary, therefore, that some one should see
Admiral Boxer, and try to interest that mild-spoken and
affable officer in our favour. When I mentioned it to Mr.
Day, he did not seem inclined to undertake the mission,
and nothing was left but for me to face the terrible Port-
Admiral. Fortunately, Captain H——, of the "Diamond,"

was inclined to be my friend, and, not a little amused with his mission, carried me right off to the Admiral. I confess that I was as nearly frightened out of my wits as I ever have been, for the Admiral's kind heart beat under a decidedly rough husk; and when Captain H—— told him that I wanted his permission for the "Nonpareil" to remain in the harbour for a few days, as there were stores on board, he let fly enough hard words to frighten any woman. But when I spoke up, and told him that I had known his son in the West Indies, he relented, and granted my petition. But it was not without more hard words, and much grumbling that a parcel of women should be coming out to a place where they were not wanted.

Now, the Admiral did not repeat this remark a few days afterwards, when he saw me attending the sick and wounded upon the sick wharf.

I remained six weeks in Balaclava, spending my days on shore, and my nights on board ship. Over our stores, stacked on the shore, a few sheets of rough tarpaulin were suspended; and beneath these—my sole protection against the Crimean rain and wind—I spent some portion of each day, receiving visitors and selling stores.

But my chief occupation, and one with which I never allowed any business to interfere, was helping the doctors to transfer the sick and wounded from the mules and ambulances into the transports that had to carry them to the hospitals of Scutari and Buyukdere. I did not forget the main object of my journey, to which I would have devoted myself exclusively had I been allowed; and very familiar did I become before long with the sick wharf of Balaclava. My acquaintance with it began very shortly after I had reached Balaclava. The very first day that I approached the wharf, a party of sick and wounded had just arrived. Here was work for me, I felt sure. With so many patients, the doctors must be glad of all the hands they could get. Indeed, so strong was the old impulse within me, that I waited for no permission, but seeing a poor artilleryman stretched upon a pallet, groaning heavily, I ran up to him at once, and eased the stiff dressings. Lightly my practised fingers ran over the familiar work, and well was I rewarded when the poor fellow's groans subsided into a restless uneasy mutter. God help him! He had been hit in the forehead, and I think his sight was gone. I stooped down, and raised some tea to his baked lips (here and there upon the wharf were rows of little pannikins containing this beverage). Then his hand touched mine, and rested there, and I heard him mutter indistinctly, as though the discovery had arrested his wandering senses—

"Ha! this is surely a woman's hand."

I couldn't say much, but I tried to whisper something about hope and trust in God; but all the while I think his thoughts were running on this strange discovery. Perhaps I had brought to his poor mind memories of his home, and the loving ones there, who would ask no greater favour than the privilege of helping him thus; for he continued to hold my hand in his feeble grasp, and whisper "God bless you, *woman*—whoever you are, God bless you!"—over and over again.

I do not think that the surgeons noticed me at first, although, as this was my introduction to Balaclava, I had not neglected my personal appearance, and wore my fa-

vourite yellow dress, and blue bonnet, with the red ribbons;
but I noticed one coming to me, who, I think, would have
laughed very merrily had it not been for the poor fellow
at my feet.  As it was, he came forward, and shook hands
very kindly, saying, "How do you do, ma'am?  Much
obliged to you for looking after my poor fellow; very glad
to see you here."  And glad they always were, the kind-
hearted doctors, to let me help them look after the sick
and wounded sufferers brought to that fearful wharf.

I wonder if I can ever forget the scenes I witnessed
there?  Oh! they were heartrending.  I declare that I
saw rough bearded men stand by and cry like the softest-
hearted women at the sights of suffering they saw; while
some who scorned comfort for themselves, would fidget
about for hours before the long trains of mules and ambulances came in, nervous lest the most trifling thing that
could minister to the sufferers' comfort should be neglected.
I have often heard men talk and preach very learnedly and
conclusively about the great wickedness and selfishness of the
human heart; I used to wonder whether they would have
modified those opinions if they had been my companions
for one day of the six weeks I spent upon that wharf, and
seen but one day's experience of the Christian sympathy
and brotherly love shown by the strong to the weak.  The
task was a trying one, and familiarity, you might think,
would have worn down their keener feelings of pity and
sympathy; but it was not so.

I was in the midst of my sad work one day when the
Admiral came up, and stood looking on.  He vouchsafed
no word nor look of recognition in answer to my salute,
but stood silently by, his hands behind his back, watching

the sick being lifted into the boats. You might have thought that he had little feeling, so stern and expression-less was his face; but once, when they raised a sufferer somewhat awkwardly, and he groaned deeply, that rough man broke out all at once with an oath, that was strangely like a prayer, and bade the men, for God's sake, take more care. And, coming up to me, he clapped me on the shoulder, saying, "I am glad to see you here, old lady, among these poor fellows;" while, I am most strangely deceived if I did not see a tear-drop gathering in his eye. It was on this same day, I think, that bending down over a poor fellow whose senses had quite gone, and, I fear me, would never return to him in this world, he took me for his wife, and calling me "Mary, Mary," many times, asked me how it was he had got home so quickly, and why he did not see the children; and said he felt sure he should soon get better now. Poor fellow! I could not undeceive him. I think the fancy happily caused by the touch of a woman's hand soothed his dying hour; for I do not fancy he could have lived to reach Scutari. I never knew it for certain, but I always felt sure that he would never wake from that dream of home in this world.

And here, lest the reader should consider that I am speaking too highly of my own actions, I must have re-course to a plan which I shall frequently adopt in the following pages, and let another voice speak for me in the kind letter received long after Balaclava had been left to its old masters, by one who had not forgotten his old com-panion on the sick-wharf. The writer, Major (then Cap-tain) R——, had charge of the wharf while I was there.

"Glasgow, Sept. 1856.

"DEAR MRS. SEACOLE,—I am very sorry to hear that you have been unfortunate in business; but I am glad to hear that you have found friends in Lord R—— and others, who are ready to help you. No one knows better than I do how much you did to help poor sick and wounded soldiers; and I feel sure you will find in your day of trouble that they have not forgotten it."

Major R—— was a brave and experienced officer, but the scenes on the sick-wharf unmanned him often. I have known him nervously restless if the people were behind-hand, even for a few minutes, in their preparations for the wounded. But in this feeling all shared alike. Only women could have done more than they did who attended to this melancholy duty; and they, not because their hearts could be softer, but because their hands are moulded for this work.

But it must not be supposed that we had no cheerful scenes upon the sick-wharf. Sometimes a light-hearted fellow—generally a sailor—would forget his pain, and do his best to keep the rest in good spirits. Once I heard my name eagerly pronounced, and turning round, recognised a sailor whom I remembered as one of the crew of the "Alarm," stationed at Kingston, a few years back.

"Why, as I live, if this ain't Aunty Seacole, of Jamaica! Shiver all that's left of my poor timbers"— and I saw that the left leg was gone—"if this ain't a rum go, mates!"

"Ah! my man, I'm sorry to see you in this sad plight."

"Never fear for me, Aunty Seacole; I'll make the best of the leg the Rooshians have left me. I'll get at them soon again, never fear. You don't think, mess-mates"—he never left his wounded comrades alone—"that they'll think less of us at home for coming back with a limb or so short?"

"You bear your troubles well, my son."

"Eh! do I, Aunty?" and he seemed surprised. "Why, look'ye, when I've seen so many pretty fellows knocked off the ship's roll altogether, don't you think I ought to be thankful if I can answer the bo'swain's call anyhow?"

And this was the sailors' philosophy always. And this brave fellow, after he had sipped some lemonade, and laid down, when he heard the men groaning, raised his head and comforted them in the same strain again; and, it may seem strange, but it quieted them.

I used to make sponge-cakes on board the "Medora," with eggs brought from Constantinople. Only the other day, Captain S——, who had charge of the "Medora," reminded me of them. These, with some lemonade, were all the doctors would allow me to give to the wounded. They all liked the cake, poor fellows, better than anything else: perhaps because it tasted of "home."

## CHAPTER XI.

My life in Balaclava could not but be a rough one.
The exposure by day was enough to try any woman's
strength; and at night one was not always certain of repose. Nor was it the easiest thing to clamber up the steep
sides of the "Medora;" and more than once I narrowly
escaped a sousing in the harbour. Why it should be so
difficult to climb a ship's side, when a few more staves in
the ladder, and those a little broader, would make it so easy,
I have never been able to guess. And once on board the
"Medora," my berth would not altogether have suited a
delicate female with weak nerves. It was an ammunition
ship, and we slept over barrels of gunpowder and tons of
cartridges, with the by no means impossible contingency
of their prematurely igniting, and giving us no time to
say our prayers before launching us into eternity. Great
care was enjoined, and at eight o'clock every evening
Captain S—— would come down, and order all lights out
for the night. But I used to put my lantern into a deep
basin, behind some boxes, and so evaded the regulation.
I felt rather ashamed of this breach of discipline one

night, when another ammunition ship caught fire in the crowded harbour, and threatened us all with speedy destruction. We all knew, if they failed in extinguishing the fire pretty quickly, what our chances of life were worth, and I think the bravest drew his breath heavily at the thought of our danger. Fortunately, they succeeded in extinguishing the firebrand before any mischief was done; but I do not think the crew of the "Medora" slept very comfortably that night. It was said that the Russians had employed an incendiary; but it would have been strange if in that densely crowded harbour some accidents had not happened without their agency.

Harassing work, indeed, was the getting our stores on shore, with the aid of the Greek and Maltese boatmen, whose profession is thievery. Not only did they demand exorbitant sums for the carriage, but they contrived to rob us by the way in the most ingenious manner. Thus many things of value were lost in the little journey from the "Albatross" and "Nonpareil" to the shore, which had made the long voyage from England safely. Keep as sharp a look out as I might, some package or box would be tipped overboard by the sudden swaying of the boat, or passing by of one of the boatmen—of course, accidentally —and no words could induce the rascals, in their feigned ignorance of my language, to stop; and, looking back at the helpless waif, it was not altogether consolatory to see another boat dart from between some shipping, where it had been waiting, as accidentally, ready to pounce upon any such wind or waterfalls.

Still more harassing work was it to keep the things together on the shore: often in the open light of day, while I sat there (after my duties on the sick-wharf were over) selling stores, or administering medicine to the men of the Land Transport and Army Works Corps, and others, who soon found out my skill, valuable things would be abstracted; while there was no limit to the depredations by night. Of course we hired men to watch; but our choice of servants was very limited, and very often those we employed not only shut their eyes to the plunder of their companions, but helped themselves freely. The adage, "set a thief to catch a thief," answered very badly in Balaclava.

Sometimes Jew Johnny would volunteer to watch for the night; and glad I was when I knew that the honest lynx-eyed fellow was there. One night he caught a great-limbed Turk making off with a firkin of butter and some other things. The fellow broke away from Johnny's grasp with the butter, but the lad marked him down to his wretched den, behind the engineers' quarters, and, on the following morning, quietly introduced me to the lazy culprit, who was making up for the partial loss of his night's rest among as evil-looking a set of comrades as I have ever seen. There was a great row, and much indignation shown at the purpose of my visit; but I considered myself justified in calling in the aid of one of the Provost marshal's officers, and, in the presence of this most invaluable official, a confession was soon made. Beneath the fellow's dirty bed, the butter was found buried; and, in its company, a two-dozen case of sherry, which the rogue had, in flagrant defiance of the Prophet's injunction, stolen for his own private drinking, a few nights previously.

The thievery in this little out-of-the way port was

something marvellous; and the skill and ingenuity of the operators would have reflected credit upon the *élite* of their profession practising in the most civilized city of Europe. Nor was the thievery confined altogether to the professionals, who had crowded to this scene of action from the cities and islands of the Mediterranean. They robbed us, the Turks, and one another; but a stronger hand was sometimes laid on them. The Turk, however, was sure to be the victim, let who might be the oppressor.

In this predatory warfare, as in more honourable service, the Zouaves particularly distinguished themselves. These undoubtedly gallant little fellows, always restless for action, of some sort, would, when the luxury of a brush with the Russians was occasionally denied them, come down to Balaclava, in search of opportunities of waging war against society at large. Their complete and utter absence of conscientious scruples as to the rights of property was most amusing. To see a Zouave gravely cheat a Turk, or trip up a Greek street-merchant, or Maltese fruit-seller, and scud away with the spoil, cleverly stowed in his roomy red pantaloons, was an operation, for its coolness, expedition, and perfectness, well worth seeing. And, to a great extent, they escaped scatheless, for the English Provost marshal's department was rather chary of interfering with the eccentricities of our gallant allies; while if the French had taken close cognizance of the Zouaves' amusements out of school, one-half of the regiments would have been always engaged punishing the other half.

The poor Turk! it is lamentable to think how he was robbed, abused, and bullied by his friends. Why didn't

he show a little pluck? There wasn't a rough sailor, or
shrewd boy—the English boy, in all his impudence and
prejudice, flourished in Balaclava—who would not gladly
have patted him upon the back if he would but have held
up his head, and shown ever so little spirit. But the
Englishman cannot understand a coward—will scarcely take
the trouble to pity him ; and even the craven Greek could
lord it over the degenerate descendants of the fierce Arabs,
who—so they told me on the spot—had wrested Constantinople from the Christians, in those old times of which I
know so little. Very often an injured Turk would run up
to where I sat, and stand there, wildly telegraphing his
complaints against some villainous-looking Greek, or
Italian, whom a stout English lad would have shaken out
of his dirty skin in five minutes.

Once, however, I saw the tables turned. As the
anecdote will help to illustrate the relative positions
of the predatory tribes of Balaclava, I will narrate it.
Hearing one morning a louder hubbub than was usual
upon the completion of a bargain, and the inevitable
quarrelling that always followed, I went up to where
I saw an excited crowd collected around a Turk, in
whose hands a Greek was struggling vainly. This
Greek had, it seemed, robbed his enemy, but the Turk
was master this time, and had, in order to force from
the robber a confession of the place where the stolen
things were deposited (like dogs, as they were, these fellows were fond of burying their plunder), resorted to
torture. This was effected most ingeniously and simply
by means of some packthread, which, bound round the
Greek's two thumbs, was tightened on the tourniquet

principle, until the pain elicited a confession. But the Turk, stimulated to retaliation by his triumph, bagged the Greek's basket, which contained amongst other things two watches, which their present owner had no doubt stolen. Driven to the most ludicrous show of despair, the Greek was about to attempt another desperate struggle for the recovery of his goods, when two Zouaves elbowed their small persons upon the crowded stage, and were eagerly referred to by all the parties concerned in the squabble. How they contrived it, I cannot say, so prompt were their movements; but, in a very few minutes, the watches were in their possession, and going much faster than was agreeable either to Turk or Greek, who both combined to arrest this new movement, and thereby added a sharp thrashing to their other injuries. The Zouaves effected their escape safely, while the Greek, with a despair that had in it an equal share of the ludicrous and the tragic, threw himself upon the dusty ground, and tore his thin hair out by handfuls. I believe that the poor wretch, whom we could not help pitying, journeyed to Kamiesch, to discover his oppressors; but I fear he didn't gain much information there.

Had it not been for the unremitting activity of the authorities, no life would have been safe in Balaclava, with its population of villains of every nation. As it was, murder was sometimes added to robbery, and many of the rascals themselves died suspicious deaths, with the particulars of which the authorities did not trouble themselves. But the officials worked hard, both in the harbour and on shore, to keep order; few men could have worked harder. I often saw the old grey-haired Admiral about before the sun had fairly shown itself; and those of his subordinates must have been somewhat heavy sleepers who could play the sluggard then.

At length the necessary preparations to establish our store were made. We hit upon a spot about two miles from Balaclava, in advance of Kadikoi, close to where the railway engines were stationed, and within a mile of head-quarters. Leave having been obtained to erect buildings here, we set to work briskly, and soon altered the appearance of Spring Hill—so we christened our new home. Sometimes on horseback, sometimes getting a lift on the commissariat carts, and occasionally on the ammunition railway-waggons, I managed to visit Spring Hill daily, and very soon fitted up a shed sufficiently large to take up my abode in. But the difficulty of building our store was immense. To obtain material was next to impossible; but that collected (not a little was, by leave of the Admiral, gleaned from the floating rubbish in the harbour), to find workmen to make use of it was still more difficult. I spent days going round the shipping, offering great wages, even for an invalid able to handle saw and hammer, however roughly, and many a long ride through the camps did I take on the same errand. At length, by dint of hard canvassing, we obtained the aid of two English sailors, whom I nicknamed " Big and Little Chips," and some Turks, and set to work in good earnest.

I procured the Turks from the Pacha who commanded the division encamped in the neighbourhood of Spring Hill. It was decided that we should apply to him for help, and accordingly I became ambassadress on this delicate mission, and rode over to the Pacha's quarters,

Jew Johnny attending me as interpreter. I was received by the Pacha with considerable kindness and no trifling amount of formality, and after taking coffee I proceeded, through Jew Johnny, to explain the object of my visit, while his Excellency, a tall man, with a dark pleasing face, smoked gravely, and took my request into his gracious consideration.

On the following day came the answer to my request, in the persons of two curious Turkish carpenters, who were placed at our orders. After a little while, too, a Turkish officer, whom I christened Captain Ali Baba, took so great an interest in our labours that he would work like any carpenter, and with a delight and zeal that were astonishing. To see him fall back, and look smilingly at every piece of his workmanship, was a sight to restore the most severely tried temper. I really think that the good-hearted fellow thought it splendid fun, and never wearied of it. But for him I do not know how we should have managed with our other Turkish " chips "—chips of the true old Turkish block they were—deliberate, slow, and indolent, breaking off into endless interruptions for the sacred duties of eating and praying, and getting into out-of-the-way corners at all times of the day to smoke themselves to sleep.

In the midst of our work a calamity occurred, which was very nearly becoming a catastrophe. By the giving way of a dam, after some heavy rains, the little stream which threaded its silvery way past Spring Hill swelled without any warning into a torrent, which, sweeping through my temporary hut, very nearly carried us all away, and destroyed stores of between one and two hundred pounds in value. This calamity might have had a tragical issue for me, for seeing a little box which contained some things, valuable as relics of the past, being carried away, I plunged in after it, and losing my balance, was rolled over and over by the stream, and with some difficulty reached the shore. Some of Lord Raglan's staff passing our wreck on the following day, made inquiries respecting the loss we had sustained, and a messenger was sent from head-quarters, who made many purchases, in token of their sympathy.

My visit to the Turkish Pacha laid the foundation of a lasting friendship. He soon found his way to Spring Hill, and before long became one of my best customers and most frequent visitors. It was astonishing to note how completely, now that he was in the land of the Giaours, he adapted himself to the tastes and habits of the infidels. Like a Scotch Presbyterian, on the Continent for a holiday, he threw aside all the prejudices of his education, and drank bottled beer, sherry, and champagne with an appreciation of their qualities that no thirsty-souled Christian could have expressed more gratefully. He was very affable with us all, and would sometimes keep Jew Johnny away from his work for hours, chatting with us or the English officers who would lounge into our as yet unfinished store. Sometimes he would come down to breakfast, and spend the greater part of the day at Spring Hill. Indeed, the wits of Spring Hill used to laugh, and say that the crafty Pacha was throwing his pocket-hand-kerchief at Madame Seacole, widow; but as the honest fellow candidly confessed he had three wives already at home, I acquit him of any desire to add to their number.

The Pacha's great ambition was to be familiar with

the English language, and at last nothing would do but he must take lessons of me. So he would come down, and sitting in my store, with a Turk or so at his feet, to attend to his most important pipe, by inserting little red-hot pieces of charcoal at intervals, would try hard to sow a few English sentences in his treacherous memory. He never got beyond half a dozen; and I think if we had continued in the relation of pupil and mistress until now, the number would not have been increased greatly. "Madame Seacole," "Gentlemen, good morning," and "More champagne," with each syllable much dwelt upon, were his favourite sentences. It was capital fun to hear him, when I was called away suddenly to attend to a customer, or to give a sick man medicine, repeating gravely the sentence we had been studying, until I passed him, and started him with another.

Very frequently he would compliment me by ordering his band down to Spring Hill for my amusement. They played excellently well, and I used to think that I preferred their music to that of the French and English regimental bands. I laughed heartily one day, when, in compliance with the kind-hearted Anglo-Turkish Pacha's orders, they came out with a grand new tune, in which I with difficulty recognised a very distant resemblance to "God save the Queen."

Altogether he was a capital neighbour, and gave such strict orders to his men to respect our property that we rarely lost anything. On the whole, the Turks were the most honest of the nations there (I except the English and the Sardinians), and the most tractable. But the Greeks hated them, and showed their hate in every way. In bringing up things for the Pacha's use they would let the mules down, and smash their loads most relentlessly. Now and then they suffered, as was the case one day when I passed through the camp and saw my friend superintending the correction of a Greek who was being bastinadoed. It seemed a painful punishment.

I was sorry, therefore, when my friend's division was ordered to Kamara, and we lost our neighbours. But my pupil did not forget his schoolmistress. A few days after they had left the neighbourhood of Spring Hill came a messenger, with a present of lambs, poultry, and eggs, and a letter, which I could not decipher, as many of the interpreters could speak English far better than they could write it. But we discovered that the letter contained an invitation, to Mr. Day and myself, to go over to Kamara, and select from the spoil of the village anything that might be useful in our new buildings. And a few days later came over a large araba, drawn by four mules, and laden with a pair of glass-doors, and some window-frames, which the thoughtful kind Pacha had judged—and judged rightly—would be a very acceptable present. And very often the good-natured fellow would ride over from Kamara, and resume his acquaintance with myself and my champagne, and practise his English sentences.

We felt the loss of our Turkish neighbours in more ways than one. The neighbourhood, after their departure, was left lonely and unprotected, and it was not until a division of the Land Transport Corps came and took up their quarters near us, that I felt at all secure of personal safety. Mr. Day rarely returned to Spring Hill until nightfall relieved him from his many duties, and I depended chiefly upon two sailors, both of questionable character, two black servants, Jew Johnny, and my own reputation for determination and courage—a poor delusion, which I took care to heighten by the judicious display of a double-barrelled pistol, lent me for the purpose by Mr. Day, and which I couldn't have loaded to save my life.

## CHAPTER XII.

### THE BRITISH HOTEL—DOMESTIC DIFFICULTIES—OUR ENEMIES—THE RUSSIAN RATS—ADVENTURES IN SEARCH OF A CAT—LIGHT-FINGERED ZOUAVES—CRIMEAN THIEVES—POWDERING A HORSE.

SUMMER was fairly advanced before the British Hotel was anything like finished; indeed, it never was completed, and when we left the Hill, a year later, it still wanted shutters. But long before that time Spring Hill had gained a great reputation. Of course, I have nothing to do with what occurred in the camp, although I could not help hearing a great deal about it. Mismanagement and privation there might have been, but my business was to make things right in my sphere, and whatever confusion and disorder existed elsewhere, comfort and order were always to be found at Spring Hill. When there was no sun elsewhere, some few gleams—so its grateful visitors said—always seemed to have stayed behind, to cheer the weary soldiers that gathered in the British Hotel. And, perhaps, as my kind friend *Punch* said, after all these things had become pleasant memories of the past.

I

" The cold without gave a zest, no doubt,
    To the welcome warmth within ;
    But her smile, good old soul, lent heat to the coal,
    And power to the pannikin."

Let me, in a few words, describe the British Hotel.
It was acknowledged by all to be the most complete thing
there. It cost no less than £800. The buildings and
yards took up at least an acre of ground, and were as perfect as we could make them. The hotel and storehouse
consisted of a long iron room, with counters, closets, and
shelves ; above it was another low room, used by us for
storing our goods, and above this floated a large union-
jack. Attached to this building was a little kitchen, not
unlike a ship's caboose—all stoves and shelves. In addition
to the iron house were two wooden houses, with sleeping
apartments for myself and Mr. Day, outhouses for our
servants, a canteen for the soldiery, and a large enclosed
yard for our stock, full of stables, low huts, and sties.
Everything, although rough and unpolished, was comfortable and warm ; and there was a completeness about the
whole which won general admiration. The reader may
judge of the manner in which we had stocked the interior
of our store from the remark, often repeated by the officers,
that you might get everything at Mother Seacole's, from an
anchor down to a needle.

In addition, we had for our transport service four
carts, and as many horses and mules as could be kept
from the thieves. To reckon upon being in possession of
these, at any future time, was impossible ; we have more
than once seen a fair stud stabled at night-time, and on
the following morning been compelled to borrow cattle

from the Land Transport camp, to fetch our things up
from Balaclava.

But it must not be supposed that my domestic difficulties came to an end with the completion of the hotel.
True, I was in a better position to bear the Crimean cold
and rain, but my other foes were as busy as ever they had
been on the beach at Balaclava. Thieves, biped and
quadruped, human and animal, troubled me more than
ever; and perhaps the most difficult to deal with were
the least dangerous. The Crimean rats, for instance, who
had the appetites of London aldermen, and were as little
dainty as hungry schoolboys. Whether they had left Sebastopol, guided by the instinct which leads their kindred
in other parts of the world to forsake sinking ships, or
because the garrison rations offended their palates, or
whether they had patriotically emigrated, to make war
against the English larders, I do not pretend to guess;
but, whatever was their motive, it drew them in great
abundance to Spring Hill. They occasionally did us
damage, in a single night, to the tune of two or three
pounds—wasting what they could not devour. You could
keep nothing sacred from their strong teeth. When hard
pressed they more than once attacked the live sheep; and
at last they went so far as to nibble one of our black
cooks, Francis, who slept among the flour barrels. On the
following morning he came to me, his eyes rolling angrily,
and his white teeth gleaming, to show me a mangled
finger, which they had bitten, and ask me to dress it. He
made a great fuss; and a few mornings later he came
in a violent passion this time, and gave me instant notice
to quit my service, although we were paying him two

pounds a week, with board and rations. This time the
rats had, it appeared, been bolder, and attacked his head,
in a spot where its natural armour, the wool, was thinnest,
and the silly fellow had a notion that the souls of the slain
Russian soldiers had entered the bodies of the rats, and made
vengeful war upon their late enemies. Driven to such an
extremity, I made up my mind to scour the camp, in
search of a cat, and, after a long day's hunt, I came to the
conclusion that the tale of Whittington was by no means
an improbable one. Indeed, had a brisk young fellow
with a cat, of even ordinary skill in its profession, made
their appearance at Spring Hill, I would gladly have put
them in the way—of laying the foundation, at least—of a
fortune. At last I found a benefactor, in the Guards'
camp, in Colonel D——, of the Coldstreams, who kindly
promised me a great pet. well known in the camp, and
perhaps by some who may read these pages, by the name
of Pinkie. Pinkie was then helping a brother officer to
clear his hut, but on the following day a Guardsman
brought the noble fellow down. He lived in clover for a
few days, but he had an English cat-like attachment for
his old house, and despite the abundance of game, Pinkie
soon stole away to his old master's quarters, three miles
off. More than once the men brought him back to me, but
the attractions of Spring Hill were never strong enough
to detain him long with me.

From the human thieves that surrounded Spring Hill
I had to stand as sharp a siege as the Russians had in that
poor city against which we heard the guns thundering
daily; while the most cunning and desperate sorties were
often made upon the most exposed parts of my defences,

and sometimes with success. Scores of the keenest eyes and hundreds of the sharpest fingers in the world were always ready to take advantage of the least oversight. I had to keep two boys, whose chief occupation was to watch the officers' horses, tied up to the doorposts of the British Hotel. Before I adopted this safeguard, more than one officer would leave his horse for a few minutes, and on his return find it gone to the neighbourhood of the Naval Brigade, or the horse-fair at Kamicsch. My old friends, the Zouaves, soon found me out at Spring Hill, and the wiry, light-fingered, fighting-loving gentry spent much of their leisure there. Those confounded trowsers of theirs offered conveniences of stowage-room which they made rare use of. Nothing was too small, and few things too unwieldy, to ride in them ; like the pockets of clown in a pantomime, they could accommodate a well-grown baby or a pound of sausages equally well. I have a firm conviction that they stuffed turkeys, geese, and fowls into them, and I positively know that my only respectable tea-pot travelled off in the same conveyance, while I detected one little fellow, who had tied them down tight at his ankles, stowing away some pounds of tea and coffee mixed. Some officers, who were present, cut the cords, and, holding up the little scamp by the neck, shook his trowsers empty amid shouts of laughter.

Our live stock, from the horses and mules down to the geese and fowls, suffered terribly. Although we kept a sharp look-out by day, and paid a man five shillings a night as watchman, our losses were very great. During the time we were in the Crimea we lost over a score of horses, four mules, eighty goats, many sheep, pigs, and

poultry, by thieving alone. We missed in a single night
forty goats and seven sheep, and on Mr. Day's going to
head-quarters with intelligence of the disaster, they told
him that Lord Raglan had recently received forty sheep
from Asia, all of which had disappeared in the same
manner. The geese, turkeys, and fowls vanished by scores.
We found out afterwards that the watchman paid to guard
the sheep, used to kill a few occasionally. As he represented them to have died a natural death during the night,
he got permission to bury them, instead of which he sold
them. King Frost claimed his share of our stock too, and
on one December night, of the winter of 1855, killed no
less than forty sheep. It is all very well to smile at these
things now, but at the time they were heartrending
enough, and helped, if they did not cause, the ruin which
eventually overtook the firm of Seacole and Day. The
determination and zeal which besiegers and besieged
showed with respect to a poor pig, which was quietly and
unconsciously fattening in its sty, are worthy of record.

Fresh pork, in the spring of 1855, was certainly one
of those luxuries not easily obtainable in that part of the
Crimea to which the British army was confined, and when
it became known that Mother Seacole had purchased a
promising young porker from one of the ships in Balaclava,
and that, brave woman! she had formed the courageous
resolution of fattening it for her favourites, the excitement
among the frequenters of Spring Hill was very great. I
could laugh heartily now, when I think of the amount of
persuasion and courting I stood out for before I bound
myself how its four legs were to be disposed of. I learnt
more at that time of the trials and privileges of authority

than I am ever likely to experience again. Upon my
word, I think if the poor thing had possessed as many legs
as my editor tells me somebody called the Hydra (with
whom my readers are perhaps more familiar than I am)
had heads, I should have found candidates for them. As
it was, the contest for those I had to bestow was very
keen, and the lucky individuals who were favoured by me
looked after their interests most carefully. One of them,
to render mistake or misunderstanding impossible, entered
my promise in my day-book. The reader will perhaps
smile at the following important memorandum in the
gallant officer's writing :—

"Memorandum that Mrs. Seacole did this day, in the
presence of Major A—— and Lieutenant W——, promise
Captain H——, R.A., a leg of *the* pig."

Now it was well known that many greedy eyes and
fingers were directed towards the plump fellow, and considerable interest was manifested in the result of the struggle, "Mrs. Seacole *versus* Thievery." I think they had
some confidence in me, and that I was the favourite; but
there was a large field against me, which found its backers
also; and many a bet was laughingly laid on the ultimate
fate of the unconscious porker.

I baffled many a knavish trick to gain possession of the
fine fellow ; but, after all, I lost him in the middle of the
day, when I thought the boldest rogues would not have
run the risk. The shouts and laughter of some officers who
were riding down from the front first informed me of my
loss. Up they rode, calling out—"Mother Seacole! old
lady ! quick !—*the* pig's gone !"

I rushed out, injured woman that I was, and saw it all

at a glance.  But that my straw wide-awake was in the
way, I could have torn my hair in my vexation.  I rushed
to the sty, found the nest warm, and with prompt decision
prepared for speedy pursuit.  Back I came to the horsemen, calling out—" Off with you, my sons !—they can't
have got very far away yet.  Do your best to save my
bacon !"

Delighted with the fun, the horsemen dispersed, laughing
and shouting—" Stole away ! hark away !" while I ran in-
doors, turned out all my available body-guard, and started in
pursuit also.   Not half a mile off we soon saw a horseman
wave his cap ; and starting off into a run, came to a little
hollow, where the poor panting animal and two Greek
thieves had been run down. The Provost-marshal took the
latter in hand willingly, and Piggy was brought home in
triumph.   But those who had pork expectancies, hearing
of the adventure, grew so seriously alarmed at the narrow
escape, that they petitioned me to run so desperate a
hazard no longer ; and the poor thing was killed on the
following day, and distributed according to promise.  A
certain portion was reserved for sausages, which, fried
with mashed potatoes, were quite the rage at the British
Hotel for some days.  Some pork was also sent to head-
quarters, with an account of the dangers we ran from
thieves.    It drew the following kind acknowledgment
from General B——— :

" Head-Quarters.

" MY DEAR MRS. SEACOLE,—I am very much obliged to
you indeed for your pork.  I have spoken to Colonel P———
as to the police of your neighbourhood, and he will
see what arrangement can be made for the general protec-

tion of that line of road. When the high-road is finished, you will be better off. Let me know at the time of any depredations that are committed, and we will try and protect you.—I am, faithfully yours, "M. L. B——."

For the truth was—although I can laugh at my fears now—I was often most horribly frightened at Spring Hill; and there was cause for it too. My washerwoman, who, with her family, lived not half a mile from us, was with me one day, and carried off some things for the wash. On the following morning I was horrified to learn that she, her father, husband, and children—in all, seven—had been most foully murdered during the night: only one of the whole family recovered from her wounds, and lived to tell the tale. It created a great sensation at the time, and caused me to pass many a sleepless night, for the murderers were never discovered.

Whilst I am upon the subject of Crimean thievery, I may as well exhaust it without paying any regard to the chronological order of my reminiscences. I have before mentioned what I suffered from the French. One day I caught one of our allies in my kitchen, robbing me in the most ungrateful manner. He had met with an accident near Spring Hill (I believe he belonged to a French regiment lent to assist the English in road-making), and had been doctored by me; and now I found him filling his pockets, before taking "French" leave of us. My black man, Francis, pulled from his pockets a yet warm fowl, and other provisions. We kicked him off the premises, and he found refuge with some men of the Army Works Corps, who pitied him and gave him shelter. He woke them in the middle of the night, laying hands rather clumsily on everything that was removeable; and in the morning they brought him to me, to ask what they should do with him.   Unluckily for him, a French officer of rank happened to be in the store, who, on hearing our tale, packed him off to his regiment.   I gathered from the expression of the officer's face, and the dread legible upon the culprit's, that it might be some considerable time before his itch for breaking the eighth commandment could be again indulged in.

The trouble I underwent respecting a useful black mare, for which Mr. Day had given thirty guineas, and which carried me beautifully, was immense.   Before it had been many weeks in our store it was gone—whither, I failed to discover.   Keeping my eyes wide open, however, I saw " Angelina"—so I christened her—coming quietly down the hill, carrying an elderly naval officer.   I was ready to receive the unconscious couple, and soon made my claim good.   Of course, the officer was not to blame.   He had bought it of a sailor, who in his turn had purchased the animal of a messmate, who of course had obtained it from another, and so on; but eventually it returned to its old quarters, where it only remained about a fortnight.   I grew tired of looking for Angelina, and had given her up, when one day she turned up, in capital condition, in the possession of a French officer of Chasseurs.   But nothing I could say to the Frenchman would induce him to take the view of the matter I wished, but had no right to enforce.   He had bought the horse at Kamiesch, and intended to keep it.   We grew hot at last; and our dispute drew out so large an audience that the Frenchman took alarm, and tried to make off. I held on to Angelina for a little while; but at last the mare broke away from me, as Tam o' Shanter's Maggie did from the witches (I don't mean that she left me even her tail), and vanished in a cloud of dust. It was the last I ever saw of Angelina.

More than once the Crimean thievery reduced us to woeful straits. To a Greek, returning to Constantinople, we entrusted (after the murder of our washerwoman) two trunks, containing "things for the wash," which he was to bring back as soon as possible. But neither upon Greek, trunks, nor their contents did we ever set eyes again. It was a serious loss. The best part of our table-cloths and other domestic linen, all my clothes, except two suits, and all of Mr. Day's linen vanished, and had to be replaced as best we could by fresh purchases from Kamiesch and Kadikoi.

Perhaps the most ridiculous shift I was ever put to by the Crimean thieves happened when we rose one morning and found the greater part of our stud missing. I had, in the course of the day, urgent occasion to ride over to the French camp on the Tchernaya; the only animal available for my transport was an old grey mare, who had contracted some equine disease of which I do not know the name, but which gave her considerable resemblance to a dog suffering from the mange. Now, go to the French camp I must; to borrow a horse was impossible, and something must be done with the grey. Suddenly one of those happy thoughts, which sometimes help us over our greatest difficulties, entered into my scheming brains. Could I not conceal the poor mare's worst blemishes. Her colour was grey; would not a thick coating of flour from my dredger make all right? There was no time to be lost; the remedy was administered successfully, and off I started; but, alas! the wind was high and swept the skirts of my riding habit so determinedly against the side of the poor beast, that before long its false coat was transferred to the dark cloth, and my innocent *ruse* exposed. The French are proverbially and really a polite and considerate nation, but I never heard more hearty peals of laughter from any sides than those which conveyed to me the horrible assurance that my scheme had unhappily failed.

-----

## CHAPTER XIII.

### MY WORK IN THE CRIMEA.

I HOPE the reader will give me credit for the assertion that I am about to make, viz., that I enter upon the particulars of this chapter with great reluctance; but I cannot omit them, for the simple reason that they strengthen my one and only claim to interest the public, viz., my services to the brave British army in the Crimea. But, fortunately, I can follow a course which will not only render it unnecessary for me to sound my own trumpet, but will be more satisfactory to the reader. I can put on record the written opinions of those who had ample means of judging and ascertaining how I fulfilled the great object which I had in view in leaving England for the Crimea; and before I do so, I must solicit my readers' attention to the position I held in the camp as doctress, nurse, and " mother."

I have never been long in any place before I have found my practical experience in the science of medicine useful. Even in London I have found it of service to others. And in the Crimea, where the doctors were so overworked, and sickness was so prevalent, I could not be long idle; for I never forgot that my intention in seeking the army was to help the kind-hearted doctors, to be useful to whom I have ever looked upon and still regard as so high a privilege.

But before very long I found myself surrounded with patients of my own, and this for two simple reasons. In the first place, the men (I am speaking of the "ranks" now) had a very serious objection to going into hospital for any but urgent reasons, and the regimental doctors were rather fond of sending them there; and, in the second place, they could and did get at my store sick-comforts and nourishing food, which the heads of the medical staff would sometimes find it difficult to procure. These reasons, with the additional one that I was very familiar with the diseases which they suffered most from, and successful in their treatment (I say this in no spirit of vanity), were quite sufficient to account for the numbers who came daily to the British Hotel for medical treatment.

That the officers were glad of me as a doctress and nurse may be easily understood. When a poor fellow lay sickening in his cheerless hut and sent down to me, he knew very well that I should not ride up in answer to his message empty-handed. And although I did not hesitate to charge him with the value of the necessaries I took him, still he was thankful enough to be able to *purchase* them. When we lie ill at home surrounded with comfort, we never think of feeling any special gratitude for the

sick-room delicacies which we accept as a consequence of
our illness ; but the poor officer lying ill and weary in his
crazy hut, dependent for the merest necessaries of existence
upon a clumsy, ignorant soldier-cook, who would almost
prefer eating his meat raw to having the trouble of cooking
it (our English soldiers are bad campaigners), often finds
his greatest troubles in the want of those little delicacies
with which a weak stomach must be humoured into
retaining nourishment.   How often have I felt sad at the
sight of poor lads who in England thought attending early
parade a hardship, and felt harassed if their neckcloths set
awry, or the natty little boots would not retain their
polish, bearing, and bearing so nobly and bravely, trials and
hardships to which the veteran campaigner frequently
succumbed.   Don't you think, reader, if you were lying,
with parched lips and fading appetite, thousands of miles
from mother, wife, or sister, loathing the rough food by
your side, and thinking regretfully of that English home
where nothing that could minister to your great need
would be left untried—don't you think that you would
welcome the familiar figure of the stout lady whose bony
horse has just pulled up at the door of your hut, and
whose panniers contain some cooling drink, a little broth,
some homely cake, or a dish of jelly or blanc-mange—
don't you think, under such circumstances, that you would
heartily agree with my friend *Punch's* remark :—

> " That berry-brown face, with a kind heart's trace
>     Impressed on each wrinkle sly,
>   Was a sight to behold, through the snow-clouds rolled
>     Across that iron sky."

I tell you, reader, I have seen many a bold fellow's eyes

moisten at such a season, when a woman's voice and a
woman's care have brought to their minds recollections of
those happy English homes which some of them never saw
again; but many did, who will remember their woman-
comrade upon the bleak and barren heights before
Sebastopol.

Then their calling me "mother" was not, I think,
altogether unmeaning. I used to fancy that there was
something homely in the word; and, reader, you cannot
think how dear to them was the smallest thing that
reminded them of home.

Some of my Crimean patients, who were glad of me as
nurse and doctress, bore names familiar to all England, and
perhaps, did I ask them, they would allow me to publish
those names. I am proud to think that a gallant sailor, on
whose brave breast the order of Victoria rests—a more
gallant man can never wear it—sent for the doctress whom
he had known in Kingston, when his arm, wounded on the
fatal 18th of June, refused to heal, and I think that the
application I recommended did it good; but I shall let
some of my patients' letters, taken from a large bundle,
speak for me. Of course I must suppress most of their
names. Here are two from one of my best and kindest
sons.

"MY DEAR MAMMA,—Will you kindly give the bearer the
bottle you promised me when you were here this morning,
for my jaundice. Please let me know how much I am to
take of it. Yours truly,        "F. M., *C. E.*"

You see the medicine does him good, for a few days
later comes another from the same writer:—

"My dear Mrs. Seacole,—I have finished the bottle, which has done my jaundice a deal of good. Will you kindly send another by bearer. Truly yours, "F. M."

It was a capital prescription which had done his jaundice good. There was so great a demand for it, that I kept it mixed in a large pan, ready to ladle it out to the scores of applicants who came for it.

Sometimes they would send for other and no less important medicines. Here is such an application from a sick officer :—

"Mrs. Seacole would confer a favour on the writer, who is very ill, by giving his servant (the bearer) a boiled or roast fowl; if it be impossible to obtain them, some chicken broth would be very acceptable.

"I am yours, truly obliged, "J. K., 18th R. S."

Doesn't that read like a sick man's letter, glad enough to welcome any woman's face? Here are some gentlemen of the Commissariat anxious to speak for me :—

"Arthur C——, Comm. Staff Officer, having been attacked one evening with a very bad diarrhœa at Mrs. Seacole's, took some of her good medicine. It cured me before the next morning, and I have never been attacked since.—October 17th, 1855."

"Archibald R. L——, Comm. Staff, Crimea, was suffering from diarrhœa for a week or more; after taking Mrs. Seacole's good medicines for two days, he became quite well, and remained so to this day.—October 17th, 1855."

Here is Mr. M——, paymaster of the Land Transport Corps, ready with a good account of my services :—

"I certify that Madame Seacole twice cured me effectually of dysentery while in the Crimea, and also my clerk and the men of my corps, to my certain knowledge."

And some of the men shall speak for themselves :—

"Stationary Engine, December 1, 1855.

"I certify that I was severely attacked by diarrhœa after landing in the Crimea. I took a great deal of medicine, but nothing served me until I called on Mrs. Seacole. She gave me her medicine but once, and I was cured effectually.        "WM. KNOLLYS, Sergt., L.T.C."

"This is to certify that Wm. Row, L. T. C., had a severe attack of illness, and was in a short time restored to health by the prompt attention and medical skill of Mrs. Seacole, British Hotel, Spring Hill, Crimea."

Many of my patients belonged to the Land Transport and Army Works Corps. The former indeed were in my close neighbourhood, and their hospital was nearly opposite to the British Hotel. I did all I could for them, and have many letters expressive of their gratitude. From them I select the following :—

"Head-Quarters, Camp, Crimea, June 30, 1856.

"I have much pleasure in bearing testimony to Mrs. Seacole's kindness and attention to the sick of the Railway Labourers' Army Works Corps and Land Transport Corps during the winters of 1854 and 1855.

"She not only, from the knowledge she had acquired in the West Indies, was enabled to administer appropriate remedies for their ailments, but, what was of as much or more importance, she charitably furnished them with proper nourishment, which they had no means of obtaining except in the hospital, and most of that class had an objection to go into hospital, particularly the railway labourers and the men of the Army Works Corps.

"JOHN HALL,

"Inspector-General of Hospitals."

I hope that Mr. P——, of the Army Works Corps, will pardon my laying the following letter before the public :—

"DEAR MRS. SEACOLE,—It is with feelings of great pleasure that I hear you are safely arrived in England, upon which I beg to congratulate you, and return you many thanks for your kindness whilst in the Crimea.

"The bitter sherry you kindly made up for me was in truth a great blessing to both myself and my son, and as I expect to go to Bombay shortly, I would feel grateful to you if you would favour me with the receipt for making it, as it appears to be so very grateful a beverage for weakness and bowel complaints in a warm climate. With many kind regards, believe me, dear madam, your obliged servant,       "SAMUEL P——,

"Late Superintendent Army Works Corps."

Here is a certificate from one of the Army Works' men, to whose case I devoted no little time and trouble :—

"I certify that I was labouring under a severe attack of diarrhœa last August, and that I was restored to health through the instrumentality and kindness of Mrs. Seacole.

"I also certify that my fingers were severely jammed whilst at work at Frenchman's Hill, and Mrs. Seacole cured me after three doctors had fruitlessly attempted to cure them.

"And I cannot leave the Crimea without testifying to the kindness and skill of Mrs. Seacole, and may God reward her for it.          "JAMES WALLEN,
                    "5th Division Army Works Corps."

Here are three more letters—and the last I shall print —from a sailor, a soldier, and a civilian:—

"This is to certify that Wm. Adams, caulker, of H.M.S. 'Wasp,' and belonging to the Royal Naval Brigade, had a severe attack of cholera, and was cured in a few hours by Mrs. Seacole."

"I certify that I was troubled by a severe inflammation of the chest, caused by exposure in the trenches, for about four months, and that Mrs. Seacole's medicine completely cured me in one month, and may God reward her.          "CHARLES FLINN, Sergt. 3rd Co. R.S.M."

                    "Upper Clapton, Middlesex, March 2, 1856.
"DEAR MADAM,—Having been informed by my son, Mr. Edward Gill, of St. George's Store, Crimea, of his recent illness (jaundice), and of your kind attention and advice to him during that illness, and up to the time he was, by the blessing of God and your assistance, restored to health, permit me, on behalf of myself, my wife, and my family, to return you our most grateful thanks, trusting you may be spared for many years to come, in health of body and vigour of mind, to carry out your benevolent intention. Believe me, my dear madam, yours most gratefully,
                    "EDWARD GILL."

And now that I have made this a chapter of testimonials, I may as well finish them right off, and have done
with them altogether.   I shall trouble the patient reader
with four more only, which I have not the heart to omit.

"Sebastopol, July 1, 1856.

"Mrs. Seacole was with the British army in the Crimea
from February, 1855, to this time.   This excellent woman
has frequently exerted herself in the most praiseworthy
manner in attending wounded men, even in positions of
great danger, and in assisting sick soldiers by all means in
her power.   In addition, she kept a very good store, and
supplied us with many comforts at a time we much
required them.            "Wm. P———,
"Adjutant-General of the British Army
in the Crimea."

"July 1, 1856.

"I have much pleasure in stating that I am acquainted
with Mrs. Seacole, and from all that I have seen or heard
of her, I believe her to be a useful and good person, kind
and charitable.                "C. A. W———,
Lt.-Gen. Comm. of Sebastopol."

The third is from the pen of one who at that time was
more looked to, and better known, than any other man in
the Crimea.   In the 2nd vol. of Russell's "Letters from
the Seat of War," p. 187, is the following entry :—

"In the hour of their illness these men (Army Works
Corps), in common with many others, have found a kind
and successful physician.   Close to the railway, half-way

between the Col de Balaclava and Kadikoi, Mrs. Seacole, formerly of Kingston and of several other parts of the world, such as Panama and Chagres, has pitched her abode —an iron storehouse with wooden sheds and outlying tributaries—and here she doctors and cures all manner of men with extraordinary success. She is always in attendance near the battle-field to aid the wounded, and has earned many a poor fellow's blessings."

Yes! I cannot—referring to that time—conscientiously charge myself with doing less for the men who had only thanks to give me, than for the officers whose gratitude gave me the necessaries of life. I think I was ever ready to turn from the latter to help the former, humble as they might be; and they were grateful in their way, and as far as they could be. They would buy me apples and other fruit at Balaclava, and leave them at my store. One made me promise, when I returned home, to send word to his Irish mother, who was to send me a cow in token of her gratitude for the help I had been to her son. I have a book filled with hundreds of the names of those who came to me for medicines and other aids; and never a train of sick or wounded men from the front passed the British Hotel but its hostess was awaiting them to offer comforts to the poor fellows, for whose suffering her heart bled.

*Punch*, who allowed my poor name to appear in the pages which had welcomed Miss Nightingale home— *Punch*, that whimsical mouthpiece of some of the noblest hearts that ever beat beneath black coats—shall last of all raise its voice, that never yet pleaded an unworthy cause, for the Mother Seacole that takes shame to herself for

speaking thus of the poor part she bore of the trials and
hardships endured on that distant shore, where Britain's
best and bravest wrung hardly Sebastopol from the grasp
of Britain's foe :—

> " No store she set by the epaulette,
>     Be it worsted or gold lace ;
> For K. C. B. or plain private Smith,
>     She had still one pleasant face.
>
> " And not alone was her kindness shown
>     To the hale and hungry lot
> Who drank her grog and ate her prog,
>     And paid their honest shot.
>
> " The sick and sorry can tell the story
>     Of her nursing and dosing deeds ;
> Regimental M.D. never worked as she,
>     In helping sick men's needs.
>
> " Of such work, God knows, was as much as she chose
>     That dreary winter-tide,
> When Death hung o'er the damp and pestilent camp,
>     And his scythe swung far and wide.
>
> " She gave her aid to all who prayed,
>     To hungry and sick and cold ;
> Open hand and heart, alike ready to part
>     Kind words and acts, and gold.
>
>     \*      \*      \*      \*
>
> " And—be the right man in the right place who can—
>     The right woman was Dame Seacole."

Reader, now that we have come to the end of this
chapter, I can say what I have been all anxiety to tell you
from its beginning. Please look back to Chapter VIII.,
and see how hard the right woman had to struggle to
convey herself to the right place.

# CHAPTER XIV.

### MY CUSTOMERS AT THE BRITISH HOTEL.

I SHALL proceed in this chapter to make the reader acquainted with some of the customers of the British Hotel, who came there for its creature comforts as well as its hostess's medicines when need was; and if he or she should be inclined to doubt or should hesitate at accepting my experience of Crimean life as entirely credible, I beg that individual to refer to the accounts which were given in the newspapers of the spring of 1855, and I feel sure they will acquit me of any intention to exaggerate. If I were to speak of all the nameless horrors of that spring as plainly as I could, I should really disgust you; but those I shall bring before your notice have all something of the humorous in them—and so it ever is. Time is a great restorer, and changes surely the greatest sorrow into a pleasing memory. The sun shines this spring-time upon green grass that covers the graves of the poor fellows we left behind sadly a few short months ago : bright flowers grow up upon ruins of batteries and crumbling trenches, and cover the sod that presses on many a mouldering token of the old time of battle and death. I dare say that, if I went to the Crimea now, I should see a smiling landscape, instead of the blood-stained scene which I shall ever associate with distress and death; and as it is with nature so it is with human kind. Whenever I meet those who have

survived that dreary spring of 1855, we seldom talk about
its horrors; but remembering its transient gleams of sun-
shine, smile at the fun and good nature that varied its long
and weary monotony. And now that I am anxious to
remember all I can that will interest my readers, my
memory prefers to dwell upon what was pleasing and
amusing, although the time will never come when it will
cease to retain most vividly the pathos and woe of those
dreadful months.

I have said that the winter had not ended when we
began operations at the British Hotel; and very often, after
we considered we were fairly under spring's influence, our
old enemy would come back with an angry roar of wind
and rain, levelling tents, unroofing huts, destroying roads,
and handing over May to the command of General Fevrier;
But the sun fought bravely for us, and in time always dispersed the leaden clouds and gilded the iron sky, and made
us cheerful again. During the end of March, the whole
of April, and a considerable portion of May, however, the
army was but a little better off for the advent of spring.
The military road to the camp was only in progress—the
railway only carried ammunition. A few hours' rain rendered the old road all but impassable, and scarcity often
existed in the front before Sebastopol, although the
frightened and anxious Commissariat toiled hard to avert
such a mishap; so that very often to the British Hotel
came officers starved out on the heights above us. The
dandies of Rotten Row would come down riding on sorry
nags, ready to carry back—their servants were on duty in
the trenches—anything that would be available for dinner.
A single glance at their personal appearance would suffice

to show the hardships of the life they were called upon to
lead.    Before I left London for the seat of war I had been
more than once to the United Service Club, seeking to gain
the interest of officers whom I had known in Jamaica; and
I often thought afterwards of the difference between those
I saw there trimly shaven, handsomely dressed, with spot-
less linen and dandy air, and these their companions, who
in England would resemble them.    Roughly, warmly
dressed, with great fur caps, which met their beards and
left nothing exposed but lips and nose, and not much of
those; you would easily believe that soap and water were
luxuries not readily obtainable, that shirts and socks were
often comforts to dream about rather than possess, and
that they were familiar with horrors you would shudder to
hear named.    Tell me, reader, can you fancy what the
want of so simple a thing as a pocket-handkerchief is?
To put a case—have you ever gone out for the day without
one; sat in a draught and caught a sneezing cold in the
head?    You say the question is an unnecessarily unpleasant one, and yet what I am about to tell you is true,
and the sufferer is, I believe, still alive.

An officer had ridden down one day to obtain refreshments (this was very early in the spring); some nice
fowls had just been taken from the spit, and I offered one
to him.    Paper was one of the most hardly obtainable
luxuries of the Crimea, and I rarely had any to waste upon
my customers; so I called out, "Give me your pocket-
handkerchief, my son, that I may wrap it up."    You see
we could not be very particular out there; but he smiled
very bitterly as he answered, " Pocket-handkerchief,
mother—by Jove ! I wish I had one.  I tore my last shirt

into shreds a fortnight ago, and there's not a bit of it left now."

Shortly after, a hundred dozen of these useful articles came to my store, and I sold them all to officers and men very speedily.

For some time, and until I found the task beyond my strength, I kept up a capital table at the British Hotel; but at last I gave up doing so professedly, and my hungry customers had to make shift with whatever was on the premises. Fortunately they were not over-dainty, and had few antipathies. My duties increased so rapidly, that sometimes it was with difficulty that I found time to eat and sleep. Could I have obtained good servants, my daily labours would have been lightened greatly; but my staff never consisted of more than a few boys, two black cooks, some Turks—one of whom, Osman, had enough to do to kill and pluck the poultry, while the others looked after the stock and killed our goats and sheep—and as many runaway sailors or good-for-noughts in search of employment as we could from time to time lay our hands upon; but they never found my larder entirely empty. I often used to roast a score or so of fowls daily, besides boiling hams and tongues. Either these or a slice from a joint of beef or mutton you would be pretty sure of finding at your service in the larder of the British Hotel.

Would you like, gentle reader, to know what other things suggestive of home and its comforts your relatives and friends in the Crimea could obtain from the hostess of Spring Hill? I do not tell you that the following articles were all obtainable at the commencement, but many were. The time was indeed when, had you asked me for mock

turtle and venison, you should have had them, preserved
in tins, but that was when the Crimea was flooded with
plenty—too late, alas! to save many whom want had
killed; but had you been doing your best to batter Sebastopol about the ears of the Russians in the spring and
summer of the year before last, the firm of Seacole and
Day would have been happy to have served you with (I
omit ordinary things) linen and hosiery, saddlery, caps,
boots and shoes, for the outer man; and for the inner
man, meat and soups of every variety in tins (you can
scarcely conceive how disgusted we all became at last with
preserved provisions); salmon, lobsters, and oysters, also in
tins, which last beaten up into fritters, with onions, butter,
eggs, pepper, and salt, were very good; game, wild fowl,
vegetables, also preserved, eggs, sardines, curry powder,
cigars, tobacco, snuff, cigarette papers, tea, coffee, tooth
powder, and currant jelly. When cargoes came in from
Constantinople, we bought great supplies of potatoes,
carrots, turnips, and greens. Ah! what a rush there used
to be for the greens. You might sometimes get hot rolls;
but, generally speaking, I bought the Turkish bread
(*ekmek*), baked at Balaclava.

Or had you felt too ill to partake of your rough camp
fare, coarsely cooked by a soldier cook, who, unlike the
French, could turn his hand to few things but fighting,
and had ridden down that muddy road to the Col, to see
what Mother Seacole could give you for dinner, the
chances were you would have found a good joint of
mutton, not of the fattest, forsooth; for in such miserable
condition were the poor beasts landed, that once, when
there came an urgent order from head-quarters for twenty-

five pounds of mutton, we had to cut up one sheep and a half to provide the quantity; or you would have stumbled upon something curried, or upon a good Irish stew, nice and hot, with plenty of onions and potatoes, or upon some capital meat-pies. I found the preserved meats were better relished cooked in this fashion, and well doctored with stimulants. Before long I grew as familiar with the mysteries of seasoning as any London pieman, and could accommodate myself to the requirements of the seasons as readily. Or had there been nothing better, you might have gone further and fared on worse fare than one of my Welch rabbits, for the manufacture of which I became so famous. And had you been fortunate enough to have visited the British Hotel upon rice-pudding day, I warrant you would have ridden back to your hut with kind thoughts of Mother Seacole's endeavours to give you a taste of home. If I had nothing else to be proud of, I think my rice puddings, made without milk, upon the high road to Sebastopol, would have gained me a reputation. What a shout there used to be when I came out of my little caboose, hot and flurried, and called out, " Rice-pudding day, my sons." Some of them were baked in large shallow pans, for the men and the sick, who always said that it reminded them of home. You would scarcely expect to finish up your dinner with pastry, but very often you would have found a good stock of it in my larder. Whenever I had a few leisure moments, I used to wash my hands, roll up my sleeves and roll out pastry. Very often I was interrupted to dispense medicines; but if the tarts had a flavour of senna, or the puddings tasted of rhubarb, it never interfered with their consumption.

I declare I never heard or read of an army so partial to pastry as that British army before Sebastopol; while I had a reputation for my sponge-cakes that any pastry-cook in London, even Gunter, might have been proud of. The officers, full of fun and high spirits, used to crowd into the little kitchen, and, despite all my remonstrances, which were not always confined to words, for they made me frantic sometimes, and an iron spoon is a tempting weapon, would carry off the tarts hot from the oven, while the good-for-nothing black cooks, instead of lending me their aid, would stand by and laugh with all their teeth. And when the hot season commenced, the crowds that came to the British Hotel for my claret and cider cups, and other cooling summer drinks, were very complimentary in their expressions of appreciation of my skill.

Now, supposing that you had made a hearty dinner and were thinking of starting homeward—if I can use so pleasant a term in reference to your cheerless quarters—it was very natural that you should be anxious to carry back something to your hut. Perhaps you expected to be sent into the trenches (many a supper cooked by me has been consumed in those fearful trenches by brave men, who could eat it with keen appetites while the messengers of death were speeding around them); or perhaps you had planned a little dinner-party, and wanted to give your friends something better than their ordinary fare. Anyhow, you would in all probability have some good reason for returning laden with comforts and necessaries from Spring Hill. You would not be very particular about carrying them. You might have been a great swell at home, where you would have shuddered if Bond Street had seen you carrying a parcel no larger than your card-case; but those considerations rarely troubled you here. Very likely, your servant was lying crouched in a rifle pit, having "pots" at the Russians, or keeping watch and ward in the long lines of trenches, or, stripped to his shirt, shovelling powder and shot into the great guns, whose steady roar broke the evening's calm. So if you did not wait upon yourself, you would stand a very fair chance of being starved. But you would open your knapsack, if you had brought one, for me to fill it with potatoes, and halloo out, "Never mind, mother!" although the gravy from the fowls on your saddle before you was soaking through the little modicum of paper which was all I could afford you. So laden, you would cheerfully start up the hill of mud hut-ward; and well for you if you did not come to grief on that treacherous sea of mud that lay swelling between the Col and your destination. Many a mishap, ludicrous but for their consequences, happened on it. I remember a young officer coming down one day just in time to carry off my last fowl and meat pie. Before he had gone far, the horse so floundered in the mud that the saddle-girths broke, and while the pies rolled into the clayey soil in one direction, the fowl flew in another. To make matters worse, the horse, in his efforts to extricate himself, did for them entirely; and in terrible distress, the poor fellow came back for me to set him up again. I shook my head for a long time, but at last, after he had over and over again urged upon me pathetically that he had two fellows coming to dine with him at six, and nothing in the world in his hut but salt pork, I resigned a plump fowl which I had kept back for my own dinner. Off he started again, but soon came back with, "Oh, mother, I forgot all about the potatoes; they've all rolled out upon that —— road; you must fill my bag again." We all laughed heartily at him, but this state of things *had* been rather tragical.

Before I bring this chapter to a close, I should like, with the reader's permission, to describe one day of my life in the Crimea. They were all pretty much alike, except when there was fighting upon a large scale going on, and duty called me to the field. I was generally up and busy by daybreak, sometimes earlier, for in the summer my bed had no attractions strong enough to bind me to it after four. There was plenty to do before the work of the day began. There was the poultry to pluck and prepare for cooking, which had been killed on the previous night; the joints to be cut up and got ready for the same purpose; the medicines to be mixed; the store to be swept and cleaned. Of very great importance, with all these things to see after, were the few hours of quiet before the road became alive with travellers. By seven o'clock the morning coffee would be ready, hot and refreshing, and eagerly sought for by the officers of the Army Works Corps engaged upon making the great high-road to the front, and the Commissariat and Land Transport men carrying stores from Balaclava to the heights. There was always a great demand for coffee by those who knew its refreshing and strengthening qualities, milk I could not give them (I kept it in tins for special use); but they had it hot and strong, with plenty of sugar and a slice of butter, which I recommend as a capital substitute for milk. From that time until nine, officers on duty in the neighbourhood, or passing by, would look in for breakfast, and about half-past nine my sick patients began to show themselves. In the following hour they came thickly, and sometimes it was past twelve before I had got through this duty. They came with every variety of suffering and disease; the cases I most disliked were the frostbitten fingers and feet in the winter. That over, there was the hospital to visit across the way, which was sometimes overcrowded with patients. I was a good deal there, and as often as possible would take over books and papers, which I used to borrow for that purpose from my friends and the officers I knew. Once, a great packet of tracts was sent to me from Plymouth anonymously, and these I distributed in the same manner. By this time the day's news had come from the front, and perhaps among the casualties over night there would be some one wounded or sick, who would be glad to see me ride up with the comforts he stood most in need of; and during the day, if any accident occurred in the neighbour-hood or on the road near the British Hotel, the men generally brought the sufferer there, whence, if the hurt was serious, he would be transferred to the hospital of the Land Transport opposite. I used not always to stand upon too much ceremony when I heard of sick or wounded officers in the front. Sometimes their friends would ask me to go to them, though very often I waited for no hint, but took the chance of meeting with a kind reception. I used to think of their relatives at home, who would have given so much to possess my privilege; and more than one officer have I startled by appearing before him, and telling him abruptly that he must have a mother, wife, or sister at home whom he missed, and that he must therefore be glad of some woman to take their place.

Until evening the store would be filled with customers
wanting stores, dinners, and luncheons; loungers and
idlers seeking conversation and amusement; and at eight
o'clock the curtain descended on that day's labour, and I
could sit down and eat at leisure. It was no easy thing to
clear the store, canteen, and yards; but we determined upon
adhering to the rule that nothing should be sold after that
hour, and succeeded. Any one who came after that time,
came simply as a friend. There could be no necessity for
any one, except on extraordinary occasions, when the rule
could be relaxed, to purchase things after eight o'clock.
And drunkenness or excess were discouraged at Spring Hill
in every way; indeed, my few unpleasant scenes arose
chiefly from my refusing to sell liquor where I saw it was
wanted to be abused. I could appeal with a clear con-
science to all who knew me there, to back my assertion
that I neither permitted drunkenness among the men nor
gambling among the officers. Whatever happened elsewhere, intoxication, cards, and dice were never to be seen
within the precincts of the British Hotel. My regulations
were well known, and a kind-hearted officer of the Royals,
who was much there, and who permitted me to use a familiarity towards him which I trust I never abused, undertook to be my Provost-marshal, but his duties were very
light.

At first we kept our store open on Sunday from sheer
necessity, but after a little while, when stores in abundance
were established at Kadikoi and elsewhere, and the absolute
necessity no longer existed, Sunday became a day of most
grateful rest at Spring Hill. This step also met with op-
position from the men; but again we were determined, and

again we triumphed.   I am sure we needed rest.   I have
often wondered since how it was that I never fell ill or
came home " on urgent private affairs."   I am afraid that
I was not sufficiently thankful to the Providence which
gave me strength to carry out the work I loved so well, and
felt so happy in being engaged upon; but although I
never had a week's illness during my campaign, the labour,
anxiety, and perhaps the few trials that followed it, have
told upon me.   I have never felt since that time the strong
and hearty woman that I was when I braved with impu-
nity the pestilence of Navy Bay and Cruces.   It would
kill me easily now.

## CHAPTER XV.

MY FIRST GLIMPSE OF WAR—ADVANCE OF MY TURKISH FRIENDS
ON KAMARA—VISITORS TO THE CAMP—MISS NIGHTINGALE—MONS.
SOYER AND THE CHOLERA—SUMMER IN THE CRIMEA—" THIRSTY
SOULS"—DEATH BUSY IN THE TRENCHES.

IN the last three chapters, I have attempted, without any
consideration of dates, to give my readers some idea of
my life in the Crimea.   I am fully aware that I have jum-
bled up events strangely, talking in the same page, and even
sentence, of events which occurred at different times; but I
have three excuses to offer for my unhistorical inexactness.
In the first place, my memory is far from trustworthy, and
I kept no written diary; in the second place, the reader
must have had more than enough of journals and chroni-

cles of Crimean life, and I am only the historian of Spring Hill; and in the third place, unless I am allowed to tell the story of my life in my own way, I cannot tell it at all.

I shall now endeavour to describe my out-of-door life as much as possible, and write of those great events in the field of which I was a humble witness. But I shall continue to speak from my own experience simply; and if the reader should be surprised at my leaving any memorable action of the army unnoticed, he may be sure that it is because I was mixing medicines or making good things in the kitchen of the British Hotel, and first heard the particulars of it, perhaps, from the newspapers which came from home. My readers must know, too, that they were much more familiar with the history of the camp at their own firesides, than we who lived in it. Just as a spectator seeing one of the battles from a hill, as I did the Tchernaya, knows more about it than the combatant in the valley below, who only thinks of the enemy whom it is his immediate duty to repel; so you, through the valuable aid of the cleverest man in the whole camp, read in the *Times'* columns the details of that great campaign, while we, the actors in it, had enough to do to discharge our own duties well, and rarely concerned ourselves in what seemed of such importance to you. And so very often a desperate skirmish or hard-fought action, the news of which created so much sensation in England, was but little regarded at Spring Hill.

My first experience of battle was pleasant enough. Before we had been long at Spring Hill, Omar Pasha got something for his Turks to do, and one fine morning they were marched away towards the Russian outposts on the road to Baidar. I accompanied them on horseback, and enjoyed the sight amazingly. English and French cavalry preceded the Turkish infantry over the plain yet full of memorials of the terrible Light Cavalry charge a few months before; and while one detachment of the Turks made a reconnaissance to the right of the Tchernaya, another pushed their way up the hill, towards Kamara, driving in the Russian outposts, after what seemed but a slight resistance. It was very pretty to see them advance, and to watch how every now and then little clouds of white smoke puffed up from behind bushes and the crests of hills, and were answered by similar puffs from the long line of busy skirmishers that preceded the main body. This was my first experience of actual battle, and I felt that strange excitement which I do not remember on future occasions, coupled with an earnest longing to see more of warfare, and to share in its hazards. It was not long before my wish was gratified.

I do not know much of the second bombardment of Sebastopol in the month of April, although I was as assiduous as I could be in my attendance at Cathcart's Hill. I could judge of its severity by the long trains of wounded which passed the British Hotel. I had a stretcher laid near the door, and very often a poor fellow was laid upon it, outwearied by the terrible conveyance from the front.

After this unsuccessful bombardment, it seemed to us that there was a sudden lull in the progress of the siege; and other things began to interest us. There were several arrivals to talk over. Miss Nightingale came to supervise the Balaclava hospitals, and, before long, she had practical experience of Crimean fever. After her, came the Duke of Newcastle, and the great high priest of the mysteries of cookery, Mons. Alexis Soyer. He was often at Spring Hill, with the most smiling of faces and in the most gorgeous of irregular uniforms, and never failed to praise my soups and dainties. I always flattered myself that I was his match, and with our West Indian dishes could of course beat him hollow, and more than once I challenged him to a trial of skill; but the gallant Frenchman only shrugged his shoulders, and disclaimed my challenge with many flourishes of his jewelled hands, declaring that Madame proposed a contest where victory would cost him his reputation for gallantry, and be more disastrous than defeat. And all because I was a woman, forsooth. What nonsense to talk like that, when I was doing the work of half a dozen men. Then he would laugh and declare that, when our campaigns were over, we would render rivalry impossible, by combining to open the first restaurant in Europe. There was always fun in the store when the good-natured Frenchman was there.

One dark, tempestuous night, I was knocked up by the arrival of other visitors. These were the first regiment of Sardinian Grenadiers, who, benighted on their way to the position assigned them, remained at Spring Hill until the morning. We soon turned out our staff, and lighted up the store, and entertained the officers as well as we could inside, while the soldiers bivouacked in the yards around. Not a single thing was stolen or disturbed that night, although they had many opportunities. We all admired and liked the Sardinians; they were honest, well-disciplined fellows, and I wish there had been no worse men or soldiers in the Crimea.

As the season advanced many visitors came to the
Crimea from all parts of the world, and many of them were
glad to make Spring Hill their head-quarters. We should
have been better off if some of them had spared us this
compliment. A Captain St. Clair, for instance—who could
doubt any one with such a name?—stayed some time with
us, had the best of everything, and paid us most honourably
with one bill upon his agents, while we cashed another to
provide him with money for his homeward route. He was
an accomplished fellow, and I really liked him; but, unfortunately for us, he was a swindler.

I saw much of another visitor to the camp in the
Crimea—an old acquaintance of mine with whom I had
had many a hard bout in past times—the cholera. There
were many cases in the hospital of the Land Transport
Corps opposite, and I prescribed for many others personally. The raki sold in too many of the stores in Balaclava and Kadikoi was most pernicious; and although the
authorities forbade the sutlers to sell, it under heavy penal-
ties, it found its way into the camp in large quantities.

During May, and while preparations were being made
for the third great bombardment of the ill-fated city,
summer broke beautifully, and the weather, chequered
occasionally by fitful intervals of cold and rain, made us
all cheerful. You would scarcely have believed that the
happy, good-humoured, and jocular visitors to the British
Hotel were the same men who had a few weeks before
ridden gloomily through the muddy road to its door. It
was a period of relaxation, and they all enjoyed it.
Amusement was the order of the day. Races, dog-hunts,
cricket-matches, and dinner-parties were eagerly indulged

in, and in all I could be of use to provide the good cheer which was so essential a part of these entertainments; and when the warm weather came in all its intensity, and I took to manufacturing cooling beverages for my friends and customers, my store was always full. To please all was somewhat difficult, and occasionally some of them were scarcely so polite as they should have been to a perplexed hostess, who could scarcely be expected to remember that Lieutenant A. had bespoken his sangaree an instant before Captain B. and his friends had ordered their claret cup.

In anticipation of the hot weather, I had laid in a large stock of raspberry vinegar, which, properly managed, helps to make a pleasant drink; and there was a great demand for sangaree, claret, and cider cups, the cups being battered pewter pots. Would you like, reader, to know my recipe for the favourite claret cup? It is simple enough. Claret, water, lemon-peel, sugar, nutmeg, and—ice—yes, ice, but not often and not for long, for the eager officers soon made an end of it. Sometimes there were dinner-parties at Spring Hill, but of these more hereafter. At one of the earliest, when the *Times* correspondent was to be present, I rode down to Kadikoi, bought some calico and cut it up into table napkins. They all laughed very heartily, and thought perhaps of a few weeks previously, when every available piece of linen in the camp would have been snapped up for pocket-handkerchiefs.

But the reader must not forget that all this time, although there might be only a few short and sullen roars of the great guns by day, few nights passed without some fighting in the trenches; and very often the news of the morning would be that one or other of those I knew had fallen. These tidings often saddened me, and when I awoke in the night and heard the thunder of the guns fiercer than usual, I have quite dreaded the dawn which might usher in bad news.

The deaths in the trenches touched me deeply, perhaps for this reason. It was very usual, when a young officer was ordered into the trenches, for him to ride down to Spring Hill to dine, or obtain something more than his ordinary fare to brighten his weary hours in those fearful ditches. They seldom failed on these occasions to shake me by the hand at parting, and sometimes would say, "You see, Mrs. Seacole, I can't say good-bye to the dear ones at home, so I'll bid you good-bye for them. Perhaps you'll see them some day, and if the Russians should knock me over, mother, just tell them I thought of them all—will you?" And although all this might be said in a light-hearted manner, it was rather solemn. I felt it to be so, for I never failed (although who was I, that I should preach?) to say something about God's providence and relying upon it; and they were very good. No army of parsons could be much better than my sons. They would listen very gravely, and shake me by the hand again, while I felt that there was nothing in the world I would not do for them. Then very often the men would say, "I'm going in with my master to-night, Mrs. Seacole; come and look after him, if he's hit;" and so often as this happened I would pass the night restlessly, awaiting with anxiety the morning, and yet dreading to hear the news it held in store for me. I used to think it was like having a large family of children ill with fever, and dreading to hear which one had passed away in the night.

And as often as the bad news came, I thought it my duty to ride up to the hut of the sufferer and do my woman's work. But I felt it deeply. How could it be otherwise? There was one poor boy in the Artillery, with blue eyes and light golden hair, whom I nursed through a long and weary sickness, borne with all a man's spirit, and whom I grew to love like a fond old-fashioned mother. I thought if ever angels watched over any life, they would shelter his; but one day, but a short time after he had left his sick-bed, he was struck down on his battery, working like a young hero. It was a long time before I could banish from my mind the thought of him as I saw him last, the yellow hair, stiff and stained with his life-blood, and the blue eyes closed in the sleep of death. Of course, I saw him buried, as I did poor H—— V——, my old Jamaica friend, whose kind face was so familiar to me of old. Another good friend I mourned bitterly—Captain B——, of the Coldstreams—a great cricketer. He had been with me on the previous evening, had seemed dull, but had supped at my store, and on the following morning a brother officer told me he was shot dead while setting his pickets, which made me ill and unfit for work for the whole day. Mind you, a day was a long time to give to sorrow in the Crimea.

I could give many other similar instances, but why should I sadden myself or my readers? Others have described the horrors of those fatal trenches; but their real history has never been written, and perhaps it is as well that so harrowing a tale should be left in oblivion. Such anecdotes as the following were very current in the Camp, but I have no means of answering for its truth. Two ser-

geants met in the trenches, who had been schoolmates in
their youth; years had passed since they set out for the
battle of life by different roads, and now they met again
under the fire of a common enemy. With one impulse
they started forward to exchange the hearty hand-shake
and the mutual greetings, and while their hands were still
clasped, a chance shot killed both.

———

## CHAPTER XVI.

UNDER FIRE ON THE FATAL 18TH OF JUNE—BEFORE THE REDAN—AT
THE CEMETERY—THE ARMISTICE—DEATHS AT HEAD-QUARTERS—
DEPRESSION IN THE CAMP—PLENTY IN THE CRIMEA—THE PLAGUE
OF FLIES—UNDER FIRE AT THE BATTLE OF THE TCHERNAYA—WORK
ON THE FIELD—MY PATIENTS.

BEFORE I left the Crimea to return to England, the Adjutant-General of the British Army gave me a testimonial,
which the reader has already read in Chapter XIV., in
which he stated that I had "frequently exerted myself in
the most praiseworthy manner in attending wounded men,
even in positions of great danger." The simple meaning of
this sentence is that, in the discharge of what I conceived
to be my duty, I was frequently "under fire." Now I
am far from wishing to speak of this fact with any vanity
or pride, because, after all, one soon gets accustomed to it,
and it fails at last to create more than temporary uneasiness. Indeed, after Sebastopol was ours, you might often
see officers and men strolling coolly, even leisurely, across

and along those streets, exposed to the enemy's fire, when a little haste would have carried them beyond the reach of danger.' The truth was, I believe, they had grown so habituated to being in peril from shot or shell, that they rather liked the sensation, and found it difficult to get on without a little gratuitous excitement and danger.

But putting aside the great engagements, where I underwent considerable peril, one could scarcely move about the various camps without some risk. The Russians had, it seemed, sunk great ships' guns into the earth, from which they fired shot and shell at a very long range, which came tumbling and plunging between, and sometimes into the huts and tents, in a very unwieldy and generally harmless fashion. Once when I was riding through the camp of the Rifles, a round shot came plunging towards me, and before I or the horse had time to be much frightened, the ugly fellow buried itself in the earth, with a heavy "thud," a little distance in front of us.

In the first week of June, the third bombardment of Sebastopol opened, and the Spring Hill visitors had plenty to talk about. Many were the surmises as to when the assault would take place, of the success of which nobody entertained a doubt. Somehow or other, important secrets oozed out in various parts of the camp, which the Russians would have given much to know, and one of these places was the British Hotel. Some such whispers were afloat on the evening of Sunday the 17th of June, and excited me strangely. Any stranger not in my secret would have considered that my conduct fully justified my partner, Mr. Day, in sending me home, as better fitted for a cell in Bedlam than the charge of an hotel in the Crimea. I never remember feeling more excited or more restless than upon that day, and no sooner had night fairly closed in upon us than, instead of making preparations for bed, this same stranger would have seen me wrap up—the nights were still cold—and start off for a long walk to Cathcart's Hill, three miles and a half away. I stayed there until past midnight, but when I returned home, there was no rest for me; for I had found out that, in the stillness of the night, many regiments were marching down to the trenches, and that the dawn of day would be the signal that should let them loose upon the Russians. The few hours still left before daybreak, were made the most of at Spring Hill. We were all busily occupied in cutting bread and cheese and sandwiches, packing up fowls, tongues, and ham, wine and spirits, while I carefully filled the large bag, which I always carried into the field slung across my shoulder, with lint, bandages, needles, thread, and medicines; and soon after daybreak everything was ready packed upon two mules, in charge of my steadiest lad, and, I leading the way on horseback, the little cavalcade left the British Hotel before the sun of the fatal 18th of June had been many hours old.

It was not long before our progress was arrested by the cavalry pickets closely stationed to stop all stragglers and spectators from reaching the scene of action. But after a slight parley and when they found out who I was, and how I was prepared for the day's work, the men raised a shout for me, and, with their officer's sanction, allowed me to pass. So I reached Cathcart's Hill crowded with non-combatants, and, leaving there the mules, loaded myself with what provisions I could carry, and—it was a work of

no little difficulty and danger—succeeded in reaching the
reserves of Sir Henry Barnard's division, which was to
have stormed something, I forget what; but when they
found the attack upon the Redan was a failure, very wisely
abstained. Here I found plenty of officers who soon relieved me of my refreshments, and some wounded men
who found the contents of my bag very useful. At length
I made my way to the Woronzoff Road, where the temporary hospital had been erected, and there I found the
doctors hard enough at work, and hastened to help them
as best I could. I bound up the wounds and ministered
to the wants of a good many, and stayed there some considerable time.

Upon the way, and even here, I was "under fire."
More frequently than was agreeable, a shot would come
ploughing up the ground and raising clouds of dust, or a
shell whizz above us. Upon these occasions those around
would cry out, "Lie down, mother, lie down!" and with
very undignified and unladylike haste I had to embrace
the earth, and remain there until the same voices would
laughingly assure me that the danger was over, or one,
more thoughtful than the rest, would come to give me a
helping hand, and hope that the old lady was neither hit
nor frightened. Several times in my wanderings on that
eventful day, of which I confess to have a most confused
remembrance, only knowing that I looked after many
wounded men, I was ordered back, but each time my
bag of bandages and comforts for the wounded proved my
passport. While at the hospital I was chiefly of use
looking after those, who, either from lack of hands or
because their hurts were less serious, had to wait, pained

and weary, until the kind-hearted doctors—who, however, *looked* more like murderers—could attend to them. And the grateful words and smile which rewarded me for binding up a wound or giving cooling drink was a pleasure worth risking life for at any time. It was here that I received my only wound during the campaign. I threw myself too hastily on the ground, in obedience to the command of those around me, to escape a threatening shell, and fell heavily on the thumb of my right hand, dislocating it. It was bound up on the spot and did not inconvenience me much, but it has never returned to its proper shape.

After this, first washing my hands in some sherry from lack of water, I went back to Cathcart's Hill, where I found my horse, and heard that the good-for-nothing lad, either frightened or tired of waiting, had gone away with the mules. I had to ride three miles after him, and then the only satisfaction I had arose from laying my horse-whip about his shoulders. After that, working my way round, how I can scarcely tell, I got to the extreme left attack, where General Eyre's division had been hotly engaged all day, and had suffered severely. I left my horse in charge of some men, and with no little difficulty, and at no little risk, crept down to where some wounded men lay, with whom I left refreshments. And then—it was growing late—I started for Spring Hill, where I heard all about the events of the luckless day from those who had seen them from posts of safety, while I, who had been in the midst of it all day, knew so little.

On the following day some Irishmen of the 8th Royals brought me, in token of my having been among them, a Russian woman's dress and a poor pigeon, which they had brought away from one of the houses in the suburb where their regiment suffered so severely.

But that evening of the 18th of June was a sad one, and the news that came in of those that had fallen were most heartrending. Both the leaders, who fell so gloriously before the Redan, had been very good to the mistress of Spring Hill. But a few days before the 18th, Col. Y—— had merrily declared that I should have a silver salver to hand about things upon, instead of the poor shabby one I had been reduced to; while Sir John C—— had been my kind patron for some years. It was in my house in Jamaica that Lady C—— had once lodged when her husband was stationed in that island. And when the recall home came, Lady C——, who, had she been like most women, would have shrunk from any exertion, declared that she was a soldier's wife and would accompany him. Fortunately the "Blenheim" was detained in the roads a few days after the time expected for her departure, and I put into its father's arms a little Scotchman, born within sight of the blue hills of Jamaica. And yet with these at home, the brave general—as I read in the *Times* a few weeks later—displayed a courage amounting to rashness, and, sending away his aides-de-camp, rushed on to a certain death.

On the following day, directly I heard of the armistice, I hastened to the scene of action, anxious to see once more the faces of those who had been so kind to me in life. That battle-field was a fearful sight for a woman to witness, and if I do not pray God that I may never see its like again, it is because I wish to be useful all my life, and it is in scenes of horror and distress that a woman can do so much. It was late in the afternoon, not, I think,

until half-past four, that the Russians brought over the
bodies of the two leaders of yesterday's assault. They
had stripped Sir John of epaulettes, sword, and boots.
Ah! how my heart felt for those at home who would so
soon hear of this day's fatal work. It was on the following
day, I think, that I saw them bury him near Cathcart's
Hill, where his tent had been pitched. If I had been in
the least humour for what was ludicrous, the looks and
curiosity of the Russians who saw me during the armistice
would have afforded me considerable amusement. I
wonder what rank they assigned me.

How true it is, as somebody has said, that misfortunes
never come singly. N.B. Pleasures often do. For while
we were dull enough at this great trouble, we had cholera
raging around us, carrying off its victims of all ranks.
There was great distress in the Sardinian camp on this
account, and I soon lost another good customer, General
E——, carried off by the same terrible plague. Before
Mrs. E—— left the Crimea, she sent several useful things,
kept back from the sale of the general's effects. At this
sale I wanted to buy a useful waggon, but did not like to
bid against Lord W——, who purchased it; but (I tell
this anecdote to show how kind they all were to me) when
his lordship heard of this he sent it over to Spring Hill,
with a message that it was mine for a far lower price than
he had given for it. And since my return home I have
had to thank the same nobleman for still greater favours.
But who, indeed, has not been kind to me?

Within a week after General E——'s death, a still
greater calamity happened. Lord Raglan died—that great
soldier who had such iron courage, with the gentle smile

and kind word that always show the good man. I was familiar enough with his person; for, although people did not know it in England, he was continually in the saddle looking after his suffering men, and scheming plans for their benefit. And the humblest soldier will remember that, let who might look stern and distant, the first man in the British army ever had a kind word to give him.

During the time he was ill I was at head-quarters several times, and once his servants allowed me to peep into the room where their master lay. I do not think they knew that he was dying, but they seemed very sad and low —far more so than he for whom they feared. And on the day of his funeral I was there again. I never saw such heartfelt gloom as that which brooded on the faces of his attendants; but it was good to hear how they all, even the humblest, had some kind memory of the great general whom Providence had called from his post at such a season of danger and distress. And once again they let me into the room in which the coffin lay, and I timidly stretched out my hand and touched a corner of the union-jack which lay upon it; and then I watched it wind its way through the long lines of soldiery towards Kamiesch, while, ever and anon, the guns thundered forth in sorrow, not in anger. And for days after I could not help thinking of the "Caradoc," which was ploughing its way through the sunny sea with its sad burden.

It was not in the nature of the British army to remain long dull, and before very long we went on gaily as ever, forgetting the terrible 18th of June, or only remembering it to look forward to the next assault compensating for all. And once more the British Hotel was filled with a busy

M

throng, and laughter and fun re-echoed through its iron rafters. Nothing of consequence was done in the front for weeks, possibly because Mr. Russell was taking holiday, and would not return until August.

About this time the stores of the British Hotel were well filled, not only with every conceivable necessary of life, but with many of its most expensive luxuries. It was at this period that you could have asked for few things that I could not have supplied you with on the spot, or obtained for you, if you had a little patience and did not mind a few weeks' delay. Not only Spring Hill and Kadikoi, which—a poor place enough when we came—had grown into a town of stores, and had its market regulations and police, but the whole camp shared in this unusual plenty. Even the men could afford to despise salt meat and pork, and fed as well, if not better, than if they had been in quarters at home. And there were coffee-houses and places of amusement opened at Balaclava, and balls given in some of them, which raised my temper to an unwonted pitch, because I foresaw the dangers which they had for the young and impulsive; and sure enough they cost several officers their commissions. Right glad was I one day when the great purifier, Fire, burnt down the worst of these places and ruined its owner, a bad Frenchwoman. And the railway was in full work, and the great road nearly finished, and the old one passable, and the mules and horses looked in such fair condition, that you would scarcely have believed Farrier C——, of the Land Transport Corps, who would have told you then, and will tell you now, that he superintended, on one bleak morning of February, not six months agone, the task of throwing the corpses of one hundred and eight mules over the cliffs at Karanyi into the Black Sea beneath.

Of course the summer introduced its own plagues, and among the worst of these were the flies. I shall never forget those Crimean flies, and most sincerely hope that, like the Patagonians, they are only to be found in one part of the world. Nature must surely have intended them for blackbeetles, and accidentally given them wings. There was no exterminating them—no thinning them—no escaping from them by night or by day. One of my boys confined himself almost entirely to laying baits and traps for their destruction, and used to boast that he destroyed them at the rate of a gallon a day; but I never noticed any perceptible decrease in their powers of mischief and annoyance. The officers in the front suffered terribly from them. One of my kindest customers, a lieutenant serving in the Royal Naval Brigade, who was a close relative of the Queen, whose uniform he wore, came to me in great perplexity. He evidently considered the fly nuisance the most trying portion of the campaign, and of far more consequence than the Russian shot and shell. "Mami," he said (he had been in the West Indies, and so called me by the familiar term used by the Creole children), "Mami, these flies respect nothing. Not content with eating my prog, they set to at night and make a supper of me," and his face showed traces of their attacks. "Confound them, they'll kill me, mami; they're everywhere, even in the trenches, and you'd suppose they wouldn't care to go there from choice. What can you do for me, mami?"

Not much; but I rode down to Mr. B——'s store, at Kadikoi, where I was lucky in being able to procure a piece of muslin, which I pinned up (time was too precious to allow me to use needle and thread) into a mosquito net, with which the prince was delighted. He fell ill later in the summer, when I went up to his quarters and did all I could for him.

As the summer wore on, busily passed by all of us at the British Hotel, rumours stronger than ever were heard of a great battle soon to be fought by the reinforcements which were known to have joined the Russian army. And I think that no one was much surprised when one pleasant August morning, at early dawn, heavy firing was heard towards the French position on the right, by the Tchernaya, and the stream of troops and on-lookers poured from all quarters in that direction. Prepared and loaded as usual, I was soon riding in the same direction, and saw the chief part of the morning's battle. I saw the Russians cross and recross the river. I saw their officers cheer and wave them on in the coolest, bravest manner, until they were shot down by scores. I was near enough to hear at times, in the lull of artillery, and above the rattle of the musketry, the excited cheers which told of a daring attack or a successful repulse ; and beneath where I stood I could see— what the Russians could not—steadily drawn up, quiet and expectant, the squadrons of English and French cavalry, calmly yet impatiently waiting until the Russians' partial success should bring their sabres into play. But the contingency never happened, and we saw the Russians fall slowly back in good order, while the dark-plumed Sardinians and red-pantalooned French spread out in pursuit, and formed a picture so excitingly beautiful that we forgot the suffering and death they left behind.

And then I descended with the rest into the field of battle.

It was a fearful scene; but why repeat this remark. All death is trying to witness—even that of the good man who lays down his life hopefully and peacefully; but on the battle-field, when the poor body is torn and rent in hideous ways, and the scared spirit struggles to loose itself from the still strong frame that holds it tightly to the last, death is fearful indeed. It had come peacefully enough to some. They lay with half-opened eyes, and a quiet smile about the lips that showed their end to have been painless; others it had arrested in the heat of passion, and frozen on their pallid faces a glare of hatred and defiance that made your warm blood run cold. But little time had we to think of the dead, whose business it was to see after the dying, who might yet be saved. The ground was thickly cumbered with the wounded, some of them calm and resigned, others impatient and restless, a few filling the air with their cries of pain—all wanting water, and grateful to those who administered it, and more substantial comforts. You might see officers and strangers, visitors to the camp, riding about the field on this errand of mercy. And this, although—surely it could not have been intentional—Russian guns still played upon the scene of action. There were many others there, bent on a more selfish task. The plunderers were busy everywhere. It was marvellous to see how eagerly the French stripped the dead of what was valuable, not always, in their brutal work, paying much regard to the presence of a lady. Some of the officers, when I complained rather angrily, laughed, and said it was spoiling the Egyptians; but I *do* think the

Israelites spared their enemies those garments, which, perhaps, were not so unmentionable in those days as they have since become.

I attended to the wounds of many French and Sardinians, and helped to lift them into the ambulances, which came tearing up to the scene of action. I derived no little gratification from being able to dress the wounds of several Russians; indeed, they were as kindly treated as the others. One of them was badly shot in the lower jaw, and was beyond my or any human skill. Incautiously I inserted my finger into his mouth to feel where the ball had lodged, and his teeth closed upon it, in the agonies of death, so tightly that I had to call to those around to release it, which was not done until it had been bitten so deeply that I shall carry the scar with me to my grave. Poor fellow, he meant me no harm, for, as the near approach of death softened his features, a smile spread over his rough inexpressive face, and so he died.

I attended another Russian, a handsome fellow, and an officer, shot in the side, who bore his cruel suffering with a firmness that was very noble. In return for the little use I was to him, he took a ring off his finger and gave it to me, and after I had helped to lift him into the ambulance he kissed my hand and smiled far more thanks than I had earned. I do not know whether he survived his wounds, but I fear not. Many others, on that day, gave me thanks in words the meaning of which was lost upon me, and all of them in that one common language of the whole world —smiles.

I carried two patients off the field; one a French officer wounded on the hip, who chose to go back to Spring Hill and be attended by me there, and who, on leav⁻ g, told us that he was a relative of the Marshal (Pelissier); the other, a poor Cossack colt I found running round its dam, which lay beside its Cossack master dead, with its tongue hanging from its mouth. The colt was already wounded in the ears and fore-foot, and I was only just in time to prevent a French corporal who, perhaps for pity's sake, was preparing to give it it's *coup de grace.* I saved the poor thing by promising to give the Frenchman ten shillings if he would bring it down to the British Hotel, which he did that same evening. I attended to it's hurts, and succeeded in rearing it, and it became a great pet at Spring Hill, and accompanied me to England.

I picked up some trophies from the battle-field, but not many, and those of little value. I cannot bear the idea of plundering either the living or the dead; but I picked up a Russian metal cross, and took from the bodies of some of the poor fellows nothing of more value than a few buttons, which I severed from their coarse grey coats.

So end my reminiscences of the battle of the Tchernaya, fought, as all the world knows, on the 16th of August, 1855.

----

## CHAPTER XVII.

INSIDE SEBASTOPOL—THE LAST BOMBARDMENT OF SEBASTOPOL — ON CATHCART S HILL — RUMOURS IN THE CAMP — THE ATTACK ON THE MALAKHOFF — THE OLD WORK AGAIN — A SUNDAY EXCURSION — INSIDE "OUR" CITY — I AM TAKEN FOR A SPY, AND THEREAT LOSE MY TEMPER — I VISIT THE REDAN, ETC.— MY SHARE OF THE "PLUNDER."

THE three weeks following the battle of the Tchernaya were, I should think, some of the busiest and most event-

ful the world has ever seen. There was little doing at
Spring Hill. Every one was either at his post, or too
anxiously awaiting the issue of the last great bombardment
to spend much time at the British Hotel. I think that I
lost more of my patients and customers during those few
weeks than during the whole previous progress of the
siege. Scarce a night passed that I was not lulled to sleep
with the heavy continuous roar of the artillery; scarce a
morning dawned that the same sound did not usher in my
day's work. The ear grew so accustomed during those
weeks to the terrible roar, that when Sebastopol fell the
sudden quiet seemed unnatural, and made us dull. And
during the whole of this time the most perplexing rumours
flew about, some having reference to the day of assault,
the majority relative to the last great effort which it was
supposed the Russians would make to drive us into the
sea. I confess these latter rumours now and then caused
me temporary uneasiness, Spring Hill being on the direct
line of route which the actors in such a tragedy must take.

I spent much of my time on Cathcart's Hill, watching,
with a curiosity and excitement which became intense, the
progress of the terrible bombardment. Now and then a
shell would fall among the crowd of on-lookers which
covered the hill; but it never disturbed us, so keen and
feverish and so deadened to danger had the excitement
and expectation made us.

In the midst of the bombardment took place the important ceremony of distributing the Order of the Bath to
those selected for that honour. I contrived to witness this
ceremony very pleasantly; and although it cost me a day,
I considered that I had fairly earned the pleasure. I was

anxious to have some personal share in the affair, so I made, and forwarded to head-quarters, a cake which Gunter might have been at some loss to manufacture with the materials at my command, and which I adorned gaily with banners, flags, etc. I received great kindness from the officials at the ceremony, and from the officers—some of rank—who recognised me; indeed, I held quite a little *levée* around my chair.

Well, a few days after this ceremony, I thought the end of the world, instead of the war, was at hand, when every battery opened and poured a perfect hail of shot and shell upon the beautiful city which I had left the night before sleeping so calm and peaceful beneath the stars. The firing began at early dawn, and was fearful. Sleep was impossible; so I arose, and set out for my old station on Cathcart's Hill. And here, with refreshments for the anxious lookers-on, I spent most of my time, right glad of any excuse to witness the last scene of the siege. It was from this spot that I saw fire after fire break out in Sebastopol, and watched all night the beautiful yet terrible effect of a great ship blazing in the harbour, and lighting up the adjoining country for miles.

The weather changed, as it often did in the Crimea, most capriciously; and the morning of the memorable 8th of September broke cold and wintry. The same little bird which had let me into so many secrets, also gave me a hint of what this day was pregnant with; and very early in the morning I was on horseback, with my bandages and refreshments, ready to repeat the work of the 18th of June last. A line of sentries forbade all strangers passing through without orders, even to Cathcart's Hill; but once more I found that my reputation served as a permit, and the officers relaxed the rule in my favour everywhere. So, early in the day, I was in my old spot, with my old appliances for the wounded and fatigued; little expecting, however, that this day would so closely resemble the day of the last attack in its disastrous results.

It was noon before the cannonading suddenly ceased; and we saw, with a strange feeling of excitement, the French tumble out of their advanced trenches, and roll into the Malakhoff like a human flood. Onward they seemed to go into the dust and smoke, swallowed up by hundreds; but they never returned, and before long we saw workmen levelling parapets and filling up ditches, over which they drove, with headlong speed and impetuosity, artillery and ammunition-waggons, until there could be no doubt that the Malakhoff was taken, although the tide of battle still surged around it with violence, and wounded men were borne from it in large numbers. And before this, our men had made their attack, and the fearful assault of the Redan was going on, and failing. But I was soon too busy to see much, for the wounded were borne in even in greater numbers than at the last assault; whilst stragglers, slightly hurt, limped in, in fast-increasing numbers, and engrossed our attention. I now and then found time to ask them rapid questions; but they did not appear to know anything more than that everything had gone wrong. The sailors, as before, showed their gallantry, and even reck-lessness, conspicuously. The wounded of the ladder and sandbag parties came up even with a laugh, and joked about their hurts in the happiest conceivable manner.

I saw many officers of the 97th wounded; and, as far

as possible, I reserved my attentions for my old regiment, known so well in my native island. My poor 97th! their loss was terrible. I dressed the wound of one of its officers, seriously hit in the mouth; I attended to another wounded in the throat, and bandaged the hand of a third, terribly crushed by a rifle-bullet. In the midst of this we were often interrupted by those unwelcome and impartial Russian visitors—the shells. One fell so near that I thought my last hour was come; and, although I had sufficient firmness to throw myself upon the ground, I was so seriously frightened that I never thought of rising from my recumbent position until the hearty laugh of those around convinced me that the danger had passed by. Afterwards I picked up a piece of this huge shell, and brought it home with me.

It was on this, as on every similar occasion, that I saw the *Times* correspondent eagerly taking down notes and sketches of the scene, under fire—listening apparently with attention to all the busy little crowd that surrounded him, but without laying down his pencil; and yet finding time, even in his busiest moment, to lend a helping hand to the wounded. It may have been on this occasion that his keen eye noticed me, and his mind, albeit engrossed with far more important memories, found room to remember me. I may well be proud of his testimony, borne so generously only the other day, and may well be excused for transcribing it from the columns of the *Times* :—" I have seen her go down, under fire, with her little store of creature comforts for our wounded men; and a more tender or skilful hand about a wound or broken limb could not be found among our best surgeons. I saw her at the

assault on the Redan, at the Tchernaya, at the fall of
Sebastopol, laden, not with plunder, good old soul! but
with wine, bandages, and food for the wounded or the
prisoners."

I remained on Cathcart's Hill far into the night, and
watched the city blazing beneath us, awe-struck at the
terrible sight, until the bitter wind found its way through
my thin clothing, and chilled me to the bone; and not till
then did I leave for Spring Hill.  I had little sleep that
night.  The night was made a ruddy lurid day with the
glare of the blazing town; while every now and then came
reports which shook the earth to its centre.  And yet I
believe very many of the soldiers, wearied with their day's
labour, slept soundly throughout that terrible night, and
awoke to find their work completed: for in the night,
covered by the burning city, Sebastopol was left, a heap of
ruins, to its victors; and before noon on the following day,
none but dead and dying Russians were in the south side
of the once famous and beautiful mistress-city of the
Euxine.

The good news soon spread through the camp.  It gave
great pleasure; but I almost think the soldiers would have
been better pleased had the Russians delayed their parting
twelve hours longer, and given the Highlanders and their
comrades a chance of retrieving the disasters of the previous
day.  Nothing else could wipe away the soreness of defeat,
or compensate for the better fortune which had befallen
our allies the French.

The news of the evacuation of Sebastopol soon carried
away all traces of yesterday's fatigue.  For weeks past I
had been offering bets to every one that I would not only

be the first woman to enter Sebastopol from the English lines, but that I would be the first to carry refreshments into the fallen city. And now the time I had longed for had come. I borrowed some mules from the Land Transport Corps—mine were knocked up by yesterday's work—and loading them with good things, started off with my partner and some other friends early on that memorable Sunday morning for Cathcart's Hill.

When I found that strict orders had been given to admit no one inside Sebastopol, I became quite excited; and making my way to General Garrett's quarters, I made such an earnest representation of what I considered my right that I soon obtained a pass, of which the following is a copy:—

" Pass Mrs. Seacole and her attendants, with refreshments for officers and soldiers in the Redan and in Sebastopol.

" GARRETT, M.G.

" Cathcart's Hill, Sept. 9, 1855."

So many attached themselves to my staff, becoming for the nonce my attendants, that I had some difficulty at starting; but at last I passed all the sentries safely, much to the annoyance of many officers, who were trying every conceivable scheme to evade them, and entered the city. I can give you no very clear description of its condition on that Sunday morning, a year and a half ago. Many parts of it were still blazing furiously—explosions were taking place in all directions—every step had a score of dangers; and yet curiosity and excitement carried us on and on. I was often stopped to give refreshments to officers and men, who had been fasting for hours. Some, on the other hand, had found their way to Russian cellars; and one body of men were most ingloriously drunk, and playing the wildest pranks. They were dancing, yelling, and singing—some of them with Russian women's dresses fastened round their waists, and old bonnets stuck upon their heads.

I was offered many trophies. All plunder was stopped by the sentries, and confiscated, so that the soldiers could afford to be liberal. By one I was offered a great velvet sofa; another pressed a huge arm-chair, which had graced some Sebastopol study, upon me; while a third begged my acceptance of a portion of a grand piano. What I did carry away was very unimportant: a gaily-decorated altar-candle, studded with gold and silver stars, which the present Commander-in-Chief condescended to accept as a Sebastopol memorial; an old cracked China teapot, which in happier times had very likely dispensed pleasure to many a small tea-party; a cracked bell, which had rung many to prayers during the siege, and which I bore away on my saddle; and a parasol, given me by a drunken soldier. He had a silk skirt on, and torn lace upon his wrists, and he came mincingly up, holding the parasol above his head, and imitating the walk of an affected lady, to the vociferous delight of his comrades. And all this, and much more, in that fearful charnel city, with death and suffering on every side.

It was very hazardous to pass along some of the streets exposed to the fire of the Russians on the north side of the harbour. We had to wait and watch our opportunity, and then gallop for it. Some of us had close shaves of being hit. More than this, fires still kept breaking out around;

while mines and fougasses not unfrequently exploded from unknown causes. We saw two officers emerge from a heap of ruins, covered and almost blinded with smoke and dust, from some such unlooked-for explosion. With considerable difficulty we succeeded in getting into the quarter of the town held by the French, where I was nearly getting into serious trouble.

I had loitered somewhat behind my party, watching, with pardonable curiosity, the adroitness with which a party of French were plundering a house; and by the time my curiosity had been satisfied, I found myself quite alone, my retinue having preceded me by some few hundred yards. This would have been of little consequence, had not an American sailor lad, actuated either by mischief or folly, whispered to the Frenchmen that I was a Russian spy; and had they not, instead of laughing at him, credited his assertion, and proceeded to arrest me. Now, such a charge was enough to make a lion of a lamb; so I refused positively to dismount, and made matters worse by knocking in the cap of the first soldier who laid hands upon me, with the bell that hung at my saddle. Upon this, six or seven tried to force me to the guard-house in rather a rough manner, while I resisted with all my force, screaming out for Mr. Day, and using the bell for a weapon. How I longed for a better one I need not tell the reader. In the midst of this scene came up a French officer, whom I recognised as the patient I had taken to Spring Hill after the battle of the Tchernaya, and who took my part at once, and ordered them to release me. Although I rather weakened my cause, it was most natural that, directly I was released, I should fly at the varlet who had caused me

this trouble; and I did so, using my bell most effectually,
and aided, when my party returned, by their riding-
whips.

This little adventure took up altogether so much time
that, when the French soldiers had made their apologies to
me, and I had returned the compliment to the one whose
head had been dented by my bell, it was growing late, and
we made our way back to Cathcart's Hill. On the way, a
little French soldier begged hard of me to buy a picture,
which had been cut from above the altar of some church
in Sebastopol. It was too dark to see much of his prize,
but I ultimately became its possessor, and brought it home
with me. It is some eight or ten feet in length, and re-
presents, I should think, the Madonna. I am no judge of
such things, but I think, although the painting is rather
coarse, that the face of the Virgin, and the heads of
Cherubim that fill the cloud from which she is descending,
are soft and beautiful. There is a look of divine calmness
and heavenly love in the Madonna's face which is very
striking; and, perhaps, during the long and awful siege
many a knee was bent in worship before it, and many a
heart found comfort in its soft loving gaze.

On the following day I again entered Sebastopol, and
saw still more of its horrors. But I have refrained from
describing so many scenes of woe, that I am loth to dwell
much on these. The very recollection of that woeful
hospital, where thousands of dead and dying had been left
by the retreating Russians, is enough to unnerve the
strongest and sicken the most experienced. I would give
much if I had never seen that harrowing sight. I believe
some Englishmen were found in it alive; but it was as

well that they did not live to tell their fearful experience.

I made my way into the Redan also, although every step was dangerous, and took from it some brown bread, which seemed to have been left in the oven by the baker when he fled.

Before many days were passed, some Frenchwomen opened houses in Sebastopol; but in that quarter of the town held by the English the prospect was not sufficiently tempting for me to follow their example, and so I saw out the remainder of the campaign from my old quarters at Spring Hill.

————

## CHAPTER XVIII.

HOLIDAY IN THE CAMP—A NEW ENEMY, TIME—AMUSEMENTS IN THE CRIMEA—MY SHARE IN THEM—DINNER AT SPRING HILL—AT THE RACES—CHRISTMAS DAY IN THE BRITISH HOTEL—NEW YEAR'S DAY IN THE HOSPITAL.

WELL, the great work was accomplished—Sebastopol was taken. The Russians had retired sullenly to their stronghold on the north side of the harbour, from which, every now and then, they sent a few vain shot and shell, which sent the amateurs in the streets of Sebastopol scampering, but gave the experienced no concern. In a few days the camp could find plenty to talk about in their novel position—and what then? What was to be done? More fighting? Another equally terrible and lengthy siege of the north? That was the business of a few at head-quarters and in council at home, between whom the electric wires flashed many a message. In the meanwhile, the real workers applied themselves to plan amusements, and the same energy and activity which had made Sebastopol a heap of ruins and a well-filled cemetery—which had dug the miles of trenches, and held them when made against a desperate foe—which had manned the many guns, and worked them so well, set to work as eager to kill their present enemy, Time, as they had lately been to destroy their fled enemies, the Russians.

All who were before Sebastopol will long remember the beautiful autumn which succeeded to so eventful a summer, and ushered in so pleasantly the second winter of the campaign. It was appreciated as only those who earn the right to enjoyment can enjoy relaxation. The camp was full of visitors of every rank. They thronged the streets of Sebastopol, sketching its ruins and setting up photographic apparatus, in contemptuous indifference of the shot with which the Russians generally favoured every conspicuous group.

Pleasure was hunted keenly. Cricket matches, pic-nics, dinner parties, races, theatricals, all found their admirers. My restaurant was always full, and once more merry laughter was heard, and many a dinner party was held, beneath the iron roof of the British Hotel. Several were given in compliment to our allies, and many distinguished Frenchmen have tested my powers of cooking. You might have seen at one party some of their most famous officers. At once were present a Prince of the Imperial family of France, the Duc de Rouchefoucault, and a certain corporal in the French service, who was perhaps the best known man in the whole army, the Viscount Talon. They ex-

pressed themselves highly gratified at the *carte,* and
perhaps were not a little surprised as course after course
made its appearance, and to soup and fish succeeded
turkeys, saddle of mutton, fowls, ham, tongue, curry,
pastry of many sorts, custards, jelly, blanc-mange, and olives.
I took a peculiar pride in doing my best when they were
present, for I knew a little of the secrets of the French
commissariat. I wonder if the world will ever know
more. I wonder if the system of secresy which has so
long kept veiled the sufferings of the French army before
Sebastopol will ever yield to truth. I used to guess something of those sufferings when I saw, even after the fall
of Sebastopol, half-starved French soldiers prowling about
my store, taking eagerly even what the Turks rejected as
unfit for human food; and no one could accuse *them* of
squeamishness. I cannot but believe that in some desks
or bureaux lie notes or diaries which shall one day be given
to the world; and when this happens, the terrible distresses
of the English army will pall before the unheard-of sufferings of the French. It is true that they carried from
Sebastopol the lion's share of glory. My belief is that
they deserved it, having borne by far a larger proportion
of suffering.

There were few dinners at Spring Hill at which the
guests did not show their appreciation of their hostess's labour by drinking her health; and at the dinner I have above
alluded to, the toast was responded to with such enthusiasm
that I felt compelled to put my acknowledgments into the
form of a little speech, which Talon interpreted to his
countrymen. The French Prince was, after this occasion,
several times at the British Hotel. He was there once

when some Americans were received by me with scarcely
that cordiality which I have been told distinguished my
reception of guests; and upon their leaving I told him—
quite forgetting his own connection with America—of my
prejudice against the Yankees. He heard me for a little
while, and then he interrupted me.

"Tenez! Madame Seacole, I too am American a little."

What a pity I was not born a countess! I am sure I
should have made a capital courtier. Witness my im-
promptu answer :—

"I should never have guessed it, Prince."—And he
seemed amused.

With the theatricals directly I had nothing to do. Had
I been a little younger the companies would very likely
have been glad of me, for no one liked to sacrifice their
beards to become Miss Julia or plain Mary Ann; and even
the beardless subalterns had voices which no coaxing could
soften down. But I lent them plenty of dresses; indeed,
it was the only airing which a great many gay-coloured
muslins had in the Crimea. How was I to know when I
brought them what camp-life was? And in addition to
this, I found it necessary to convert my kitchen into a
temporary green-room, where, to the wonderment, and
perhaps scandal, of the black cook, the ladies of the company of the 1st Royals were taught to manage their petti-
coats with becoming grace, and neither to show their
awkward booted ankles, nor trip themselves up over their
trains. It was a difficult task in many respects. Although
I laced them in until they grew blue in the face, their
waists were a disgrace to the sex; while—crinoline being
unknown then—my struggles to give them becoming

*embonpoint* may be imagined. It was not until a year later that *Punch* thought of using a clothes-basket; and I would have given much for such a hint when I was dresser to the theatrical company of the 1st Royals. The hair was another difficulty. To be sure, there was plenty in the camp, only it was in the wrong place, and many an application was made to me for a set of curls. However, I am happy to say I am not become a customer of the wigmakers yet.

My recollections of hunting in the Crimea are confined to seeing troops of horsemen sweep by with shouts and yells after some wretched dog. Once I was very nearly frightened out of my wits—my first impression being that the Russians had carried into effect their old threat of driving us into the sea—by the startling appearance of a large body of horsemen tearing down the hill after, apparently, nothing. However I discovered in good time that, in default of vermin, they were chasing a brother officer with a paper bag.

My experience of Crimean races are perfect, for I was present, in the character of cantinière, at all the more important meetings. Some of them took place before Christmas, and some after; but I shall exhaust the subject at once. I had no little difficulty to get the things on to the course; and in particular, after I had sat up the whole night making preparations for the December races, at the Monastery of St. George, I could not get my poor mules over the rough country, and found myself, in the middle of the day, some miles from the course. At last I gave it up as hopeless, and, dismounting, sat down by the roadside to consider how I could possibly dispose of the piles of sandwiches, bread, cheese, pies, and tarts, which had been prepared for the hungry spectators. At last, some officers, who expected me long before, came to look after me, and by their aid we reached the course.

I was better off at the next meeting, for a kind-hearted Major of Artillery provided me with a small bell-tent that was very useful, and enabled me to keep my stores out of reach of the light-fingered gentry, who were as busy in the Crimea as at Epsom or Hampton Court. Over this tent waved the flag of the British Hotel, but, during the day, it was struck, for an accident happening to one Captain D——, he was brought to my tent insensible, where I quickly improvised a couch of some straw, covered with the Union Jack, and brought him round. I mention this trifle to show how ready of contrivance a little campaigning causes one to become. I had several patients in consequence of accidents at the races. Nor was I altogether free from accidents myself. On the occasion of the races by the Tchernaya, after the armistice, my cart, on turning a sudden bend in the steep track, upset, and the crates, containing plates and dishes, rolled over and over until their contents were completely broken up; so that I was reduced to hand about sandwiches, etc., on broken pieces of earthenware and scraps of paper. I saved some glasses, but not many, and some of the officers were obliged to drink out of stiff paper twisted into funnel-shaped glasses.

It was astonishing how well the managers of these Crimean races had contrived to imitate the old familiar scenes at home. You might well wonder where the racing saddles and boots, and silk caps and jackets had come from; but our connection with England was very different to what

it had been when I first came to the Crimea, and many a
wife and sister's fingers had been busy making the racing
gear for the Crimea meetings. And in order that the
course should still more closely resemble Ascot or Epsom,
some soldiers blackened their faces and came out as
Ethiopian serenaders admirably, although it would puzzle
the most ingenious to guess where they got their wigs and
banjoes from. I caught one of them behind my tent in
the act of knocking off the neck of a bottle of champagne,
and, paralysed by the wine's hasty exit, the only excuse
he offered was, that he wanted to know if the officers'
luxury was better than rum.

A few weeks before Christmas, happened that fearful
explosion, in the French ammunition park, which destroyed
so many lives. We had experienced nothing at all like
it before. The earth beneath us, even at the distance of
three miles, reeled and trembled with the shock; and so
great was the force of the explosion, that a piece of stone
was hurled with some violence against the door of the
British Hotel. We all felt for the French very much,
although I do not think that the armies agreed quite so
well after the taking of the Malakhoff, and the unsuccessful
assault upon the Redan, as they had done previously. I
saw several instances of unpleasantness and collision,
arising from allusions to sore points. One, in particular
occurred in my store.

The French, when they wanted—it was very seldom—
to wound the pride of the English soldiery, used to say sig-
nificantly, in that jargon by which the various nations in
the Crimea endeavoured to obviate the consequences of
what occurred at the Tower of Babel, some time ago, " Mala-

khoff bono—Redan no bono." And this, of course, usually
led to recriminatory statements, and history was ransacked
to find something consolatory to English pride. Once I
noticed a brawny man, of the Army Works Corps, bringing
a small French Zouave to my canteen, evidently with the
view of standing treat. The Frenchman seemed mis-
chievously inclined, and, probably relying upon the good
humour on the countenance of his gigantic companion,
began a little playful badinage, ending with the taunt of
" Redan, no bono—Redan, no bono." I never saw any man
look so helplessly angry as the Englishman did. For a
few minutes he seemed absolutely rooted to the ground.
Of course he could have crushed his mocking friend with
ease, but how could he answer his taunt. All at once,
however, a happy thought struck him, and rushing up to
the Zouave, he caught him round the waist and threw him
down, roaring out, "Waterloo was bono—Waterloo was
bono." It was as much as the people on the premises could
do to part them, so convulsed were we all with laughter.

And before Christmas, occurred my first and last attack
of illness in the Crimea. It was not of much consequence,
nor should I mention it but to show the kindness of my
soldier-friends. I think it arose from the sudden commencement of winter, for which I was but poorly provided.
However, I soon received much sympathy and many
presents of warm clothing, etc.; but the most delicate
piece of attention was shown me by one of the Sappers and
Miners, who, hearing the report that I was dead, positively
came down to Spring Hill to take my measure for a coffin.
This may seem a questionable compliment, but I really
felt flattered and touched with such a mark of thoughtful

attention. Very few in the Crimea had the luxury of any better coffin than a blanket-shroud, and it was very good of the grateful fellow to determine that his old friend, the mistress of Spring Hill, should have an honour conceded to so very few of the illustrious dead before Sebastopol.

So Christmas came, and with it pleasant memories of home and of home comforts. With it came also news of home—some not of the most pleasant description—and kind wishes from absent friends. "A merry Christmas to you," writes one, "and many of them. Although you will not write to us, we see your name frequently in the newspapers, from which we judge that you are strong and hearty. All your old Jamaica friends are delighted to hear of you, and say that you are an honour to the Isle of Springs."

I wonder if the people of other countries are as fond of carrying with them everywhere their home habits as the English. I think not. I think there was something purely and essentially English in the determination of the camp to spend the Christmas-day of 1855 after the good old "home" fashion. It showed itself weeks before the eventful day. In the dinner parties which were got up—in the orders sent to England—in the supplies which came out, and in the many applications made to the hostess of the British Hotel for plum-puddings and mince-pies. The demand for them, and the material necessary to manu-facture them, was marvellous. I can fancy that if returns could be got at of the flour, plums, currants, and eggs consumed on Christmas-day in the out-of-the-way Crimean peninsula, they would astonish us. One determination appeared to have taken possession of every mind—to spend the festive day with the mirth and jollity which the changed prospect of affairs warranted; and the recollection of a year ago, when death and misery were the camp's chief guests, only served to heighten this resolve.

For three weeks previous to Christmas-day, my time was fully occupied in making preparations for it. Pages of my books are filled with orders for plum-puddings and mince-pies, besides which I sold an immense quantity of raw material to those who were too far off to send down for the manufactured article on Christmas-day, and to such purchasers I gave a plain recipe for their guidance. Will the reader take any interest in my Crimean Christmas-pudding? It was plain, but decidedly good. However, you shall judge for yourself:—"One pound of flour, three-quarters of a pound of raisins, three-quarters of a pound of fat pork, chopped fine, two tablespoonfuls of sugar, a little cinnamon or chopped lemon, half-pint of milk or water; mix these well together, and boil four hours."

From an early hour in the morning until long after the night had set in, were I and my cooks busy endeavouring to supply the great demand for Christmas fare. We had considerable difficulty in keeping our engagements, but by substituting mince-pies for plum-puddings, in a few cases, we succeeded. The scene in the crowded store, and even in the little over-heated kitchen, with the officers' servants, who came in for their masters' dinners, cannot well be described. Some were impatient themselves, others dreaded their masters' impatience as the appointed dinner hour passed by—all combined by entreaties, threats, cajolery, and fun to drive me distracted. Angry cries for the major's plum-pudding, which was to have been ready an hour ago, alternated with an entreaty that I should cook the captain's mince-pies to a turn—" Sure, he likes them well done, ma'am. Bake 'em as brown as your own purty face, darlint."

I did not get my dinner until eight o'clock, and then I dined in peace off a fine wild turkey or bustard, shot for me on the marshes by the Tchernaya. It weighed twenty-two pounds, and, although somewhat coarse in colour, had a capital flavour.

Upon New Year's-day I had another large cooking of plum-puddings and mince-pies; this time upon my own account. I took them to the hospital of the Land Transport Corps, to remind the patients of the home comforts they longed so much for. It was a sad sight to see the once fine fellows, in their blue gowns, lying quiet and still, and reduced to such a level of weakness and helplessness. They all seemed glad for the little home tokens I took them.

There was one patient who had been a most industrious and honest fellow, and who did not go into the hospital until long and wearing illness compelled him. I was particularly anxious to look after him, but I found him very weak and ill. I stayed with him until evening, and before I left him, kind fancy had brought to his bedside his wife and children from his village-home in England, and I could hear him talking to them in a low and joyful tone. Poor, poor fellow! the New Year so full of hope and happiness had dawned upon him, but he did not live to see the wild flowers spring up peacefully through the war-trodden sod before Sebastopol.

## CHAPTER XIX.

BEFORE the New Year was far advanced we all began to think
of going home, making sure that peace would soon be concluded.   And never did more welcome message come anywhere than that which brought us intelligence of the armistice, and the firing, which had grown more and more slack
lately, ceased altogether.   Of course the army did not
desire peace because they had any distaste for fighting; so
far from it, I believe the only more welcome intelligence
would have been news of a campaign in the field, but they
were most heartily weary of sieges, and the prospect of
another year before the gloomy north of Sebastopol damped
the ardour of the most sanguine.   Before the armistice
was signed, the Russians and their old foes made advances
of friendship, and the banks of the Tchernaya used to be
thronged with strangers, and many strange acquaintances
were thus began.   I was one of the first to ride down to
the Tchernaya, and very much delighted seemed the
Russians to see an English woman.   I wonder if they
thought they all had my complexion.   I soon entered
heartily into the then current amusement—that of ex-
changing coin, etc., with the Russians.   I stole a march
upon my companions by making the sign of the cross upon

my bosom, upon which a Russian threw me, in exchange
for some pence, a little metal figure of some ugly saint.
Then we wrapped up halfpence in clay, and received coins
of less value in exchange. Seeing a soldier eating some
white bread, I made signs of wanting some, and threw
over a piece of money. I had great difficulty in making
the man understand me, but after considerable pantomime,
with surprise in his round bullet eyes, he wrapped up his
bread in some paper, then coated it with clay and sent it
over to me. I thought it would look well beside my
brown bread taken from the strange oven in the terrible
Redan, and that the two would typify war and peace.
There was a great traffic going on in such things, and a wag
of an officer, who could talk Russian imperfectly, set himself to work to persuade an innocent Russian that I was his
wife, and having succeeded in doing so promptly offered to
dispose of me for the medal hanging at his breast.

The last firing of any consequence was the salutes with
which the good tidings of peace were received by army
and navy. After this soon began the home-going with
happy faces and light hearts, and some kind thoughts and
warm tears for the comrades left behind.

I was very glad to hear of peace, also, although it
must have been apparent to every one that it would cause
our ruin. We had lately made extensive additions to our
store and out-houses—our shelves were filled with articles
laid in at a great cost, and which were now unsaleable,
and which it would be equally impossible to carry home.
Everything, from our stud of horses and mules down to our
latest consignments from home, must be sold for any price ;
and, as it happened, for many things, worth a year ago

their weight in gold, no purchaser could now be found. However, more of this hereafter.

Before leaving the Crimea, I made various excursions into the interior, visiting Simpheropol and Baktchiserai. I travelled to Simpheropol with a pretty large party, and had a very amusing journey. My companions were young and full of fun, and tried hard to persuade the Russians that I was Queen Victoria, by paying me the most absurd reverence. When this failed they fell back a little, and declared that I was the Queen's first cousin. Anyhow, they attracted crowds about me, and I became quite a lioness in the streets of Simpheropol, until the arrival of some Highlanders in their uniform cut me out.

My excursion to Baktchiserai was still more amusing and pleasant. I found it necessary to go to beat up a Russian merchant, who, after the declaration of peace, had purchased stores of us, and some young officers made up a party for the purpose. We hired an araba, filled it with straw, and some boxes to sit upon, and set out very early, with two old umbrellas to shield us from the mid-day sun and the night dews. We had with us a hamper carefully packed, before parting, with a cold duck, some cold meat, a tart, etc. The Tartar's two horses were soon knocked up, and the fellow obtained a third at a little village, and so we rolled on until mid-day, when, thoroughly exhausted, we left our clumsy vehicle and carried our hamper beneath the shade of a beautiful cherry-tree, and determined to lunch. Upon opening it the first thing that met our eyes was a fine rat, who made a speedy escape. Somewhat gravely, we proceeded to unpack its contents, without caring to express our fears to one another, and quite soon enough we found them realized. How or where the rat had gained access to our hamper it was impossible to say, but he had made no bad use of his time, and both wings of the cold duck had flown, while the tart was considerably mangled. Sad discovery this for people who, although hungry, were still squeamish. We made out as well as we could with the cold beef, and gave the rest to our Tartar driver, who had apparently no disinclination to eating after the rat, and would very likely have despised us heartily for such weakness. After dinner we went on more briskly, and succeeded in reaching Baktchiserai. My journey was perfectly unavailing. I could not find my debtor at home, and if I had I was told it would take three weeks before the Russian law would assist me to recover my claim. Determined, however, to have some compensation, I carried off a raven, who had been croaking angrily at my intrusion. Before we had been long on our homeward journey, however, Lieut. C—— sat upon it, of course accidentally, and we threw it to its relatives—the crows.

As the spring advanced, the troops began to move away at a brisk pace. As they passed the Iron House upon the Col—old for the Crimea, where so much of life's action had been compressed into so short a space of time—they would stop and give us a parting cheer, while very often the band struck up some familiar tune of that home they were so gladly seeking. And very often the kind-hearted officers would find time to run into the British Hotel to bid us good-bye, and give us a farewell shake of the hand; for you see war, like death, is a great leveller, and mutual suffering and endurance had made us all friends. "My dear

Mrs. Seacole, and my dear Mr. Day," wrote one on a scrap of paper left on the counter, "I have called here four times this day, to wish you good-bye. I am so sorry I was not fortunate enough to see you. I shall still hope to see you to-morrow morning. We march at seven a.m."

And yet all this going home seemed strange and some-what sad, and sometimes I felt that I could not sympathise with the glad faces and happy hearts of those who were looking forward to the delights of home, and the joy of seeing once more the old familiar faces remembered so fondly in the fearful trenches and the hard-fought battle-fields. Now and then we would see a lounger with a blank face, taking no interest in the bustle of departure, and with him I acknowledged to have more fellow-feeling than with the others, for he, as well as I, clearly had no home to go to. He was a soldier by choice and necessity, as well as by profession. He had no home, no loved friends; the peace would bring no particular pleasure to him, whereas war and action were necessary to his existence, gave him excitement, occupation, the chance of promotion. Now and then, but seldom, however, you came across such a disappointed one. Was it not so with me? Had I not been happy through the months of toil and danger, never knowing what fear or depression was, finding every moment of the day mortgaged hours in advance, and earning sound sleep and contentment by sheer hard work? What better or happier lot could possibly befall me? And, alas! how likely was it that my pre-sent occupation gone, I might long in vain for another so stirring and so useful. Besides which, it was pretty sure that I should go to England poorer than I left it, and although I was not ashamed of poverty; beginning life again in the autumn—I mean late in the summer of life— is hard up-hill work.

Peace concluded, the little jealousies which may have sprung up between the French and their allies seemed forgotten, and every one was anxious, ere the parting came, to make the most of the time yet left in improving old friendships and founding new. Among others, the 47th, encamped near the Woronzoff Road, gave a grand parting entertainment to a large company of their French neighbours, at which many officers of high rank were present. I was applied to by the committee of management to superintend the affair, and, for the last time in the Crimea, the health of Madame Seacole was proposed and duly honoured. I had grown so accustomed to the honour that I had no difficulty in returning thanks in a speech which Colonel B—— interpreted amid roars of laughter to the French guests.

As the various regiments moved off, I received many acknowledgments from those who thought they owed me gratitude. Little presents, warm farewell words, kind letters full of grateful acknowledgments for services so small that I had forgotten them long, long ago—how easy it is to reach warm hearts!—little thoughtful acts of kindness, even from the humblest. And these touched me the most. I value the letters received from the working men far more than the testimonials of their officers. I had nothing to gain from the former, and can point to their testimony fearlessly. I am strongly tempted to insert some of these acknowledgments, but I will confine myself to one :—

"Camp, near Karani, June 16, 1856.

"MY DEAR MRS. SEACOLE,—As you are about to leave
the Crimea, I avail myself of the only opportunity which
may occur for some time, to acknowledge my gratitude to
you, and to thank you for the kindness which I, in common
with many others, received at your hands, when attacked
with cholera in the spring of 1855. But I have no language to do it suitably.

"I am truly sensible that your kindness far exceeded
my claims upon your sympathy. It is said by some of
your friends, I hope truly, that you are going to England.
There can be none from the Crimea more welcome there,
for your kindness in the sick-tent, and your heroism in the
battle-field, have endeared you to the whole army.

"I am sure when her most gracious Majesty the Queen
shall have become acquainted with the service you have
gratuitously rendered to so many of her brave soldiers, her
generous heart will thank you. For you have been an
instrument in the hands of the Almighty to preserve many
a gallant heart to the empire, to fight and win her battles,
if ever again war may become a necessity. Please to
accept this from your most grateful humble servant,

"W. J. TYNAN."

But I had other friends in the Crimea—friends who
could never thank me. Some of them lay in their last
sleep, beneath indistinguishable mounds of earth; some in
the half-filled trenches, a few beneath the blue waters of
the Euxine. I might in vain attempt to gather the wild
flowers which sprung up above many of their graves, but
I knew where some lay, and could visit their last homes

on earth. And to all the cemeteries where friends rested so calmly, sleeping well after a life's work nobly done, I went many times, lingering long over many a mound that bore the names of those whom I had been familiar with in life, thinking of what they had been, and what I had known of them. Over some I planted shrubs and flowers, little lilac trees, obtained with no small trouble, and flowering evergreens, which looked quite gay and pretty ere I left, and may in time become great trees, and witness strange scenes, or be cut down as fuel for another besieging army— who can tell? And from many graves I picked up pebbles, and plucked simple wild-flowers, or tufts of grass, as memorials for relatives at home. How pretty the cemetries used to look beneath the blue peaceful sky; neatly enclosed with stone walls, and full of the grave-stones reared by friends over friends. I met many here, thoughtfully taking their last look of the resting-places of those they knew and loved. I saw many a proud head bowed down above them. I knew that many a proud heart laid aside its pride here, and stood in the presence of death, humble and childlike. And by the clasped hand and moistened eye, I knew that from many a heart sped upward a grateful prayer to the Providence which had thought fit in his judgment to take some, and in his mercy to spare the rest.

Some three weeks before the Crimea was finally evacuated, we moved from our old quarters to Balaclava, where we had obtained permission to fit up a store for the short time which would elapse before the last red coat left Russian soil. The poor old British Hotel! We could do nothing with it. The iron house was pulled down, and

packed up for conveyance home, but the Russians got all of
the out-houses and sheds which was not used as fuel. All
the kitchen fittings and stoves, that had cost us so much,
fell also into their hands. I only wish some cook worthy
to possess them has them now. We could sell nothing.
Our horses were almost given away, our large stores of
provisions, etc., were at any one's service. It makes my
heart sick to talk of the really alarming sacrifices we made.
The Russians crowded down ostensibly to purchase, in
reality to plunder. Prime cheeses, which had cost us tenpence
a pound, were sold to them for less than a penny a pound;
for wine, for which we had paid forty-eight shillings a
dozen, they bid four shillings. I could not stand this, and
in a fit of desperation, I snatched up a hammer and broke
up case after case, while the bystanders held out their
hands and caught the ruby stream. It may have been
wrong, but I was too excited to think. There was no
more of my own people to give it to, and I would rather
not present it to our old foes.

We were among the last to leave the Crimea. Before
going I borrowed a horse, easy enough now, and rode up
the old well-known road—how unfamiliar in its loneliness
and quiet—to Cathcart's Hill. I wished once more to im-
press the scene upon my mind. It was a beautifully clear
evening, and we could see miles away across the darkening
sea. I spent some time there with my companions, point-
ing out to each other the sites of scenes we all remembered
so well. There were the trenches, already becoming indistinguishable, out of which, on the 8th of September, we
had seen the storming parties tumble in confused and
scattered bodies, before they ran up the broken height of

the Redan. There the Malakhoff, into which we had also seen the luckier French pour in one unbroken stream; below lay the crumbling city and the quiet harbour, with scarce a ripple on its surface, while around stretched away the deserted huts for miles. It was with something like regret that we said to one another that the play was fairly over, that peace had rung the curtain down, and that we, humble actors in some of its most stirring scenes, must seek engagements elsewhere.

I lingered behind, and stooping down, once more gathered little tufts of grass, and some simple blossoms from above the graves of some who in life had been very kind to me, and I left behind, in exchange, a few tears which were sincere.

A few days latter, and I stood on board a crowded steamer, taking my last look of the shores of the Crimea.

---

## CONCLUSION.

I DID not return to England by the most direct route, but took the opportunity of seeing more of men and manners in yet other lands. Arrived in England at last, we set to work bravely at Aldershott to retrieve our fallen fortunes, and stem off the ruin originated in the Crimea, but all in vain; and at last defeated by fortune, but not I think disgraced, we were obliged to capitulate on very honourable conditions. In plain truth, the old Crimean firm of Seacole and Day was dissolved finally, and its partners had to recommence the world anew. And so ended *our* campaign.

One of us started only the other day for the Antipodes, while the other is ready to take any journey to any place where a stout heart and two experienced hands may be of use.

Perhaps it would be right if I were to express more shame and annoyance than I really feel at the pecuniarily disastrous issue of my Crimean adventures, but I cannot—I really cannot. When I would try and feel ashamed of myself for being poor and helpless, I only experience a glow of pride at the other and more pleasing events of my career; when I think of the few whom I failed to pay in full (and so far from blaming me some of them are now my firmest friends), I cannot help remembering also the many who profess themselves indebted to me.

Let me, in as few words as possible, state the results of my Crimean campaign. To be sure, I returned from it shaken in health. I came home wounded, as many others did. Few constitutions, indeed, were the better for those winters before Sebastopol, and I was too hard worked not to feel their effects; for a little labour fatigues me now—I cannot watch by sick-beds as I could—a week's want of rest quite knocks me up now. Then I returned bankrupt in fortune. Whereas others in my position may have come back to England rich and prosperous, I found myself poor—beggared. So few words can tell what I have lost.

But what have I gained? I should need a volume to describe that fairly; so much is it, and so cheaply purchased by suffering ten times worse than what I have experienced. I have more than once heard people say that they would gladly suffer illness to enjoy the delights of convalescence, and so, by enduring a few days' pain, gain the tender love of relatives and sympathy of friends. And on this principle I rejoice in the trials which have borne me such pleasures as those I now enjoy, for wherever I go I am sure to meet some smiling face; every step I take in the crowded London streets may bring me in contact with some friend, forgotten by me, perhaps, but who soon reminds me of our old life before Sebastopol; it seems very long ago now, when I was of use to him and he to me.

Where, indeed, do I not find friends. In omnibuses, in river steamboats, in places of public amusement, in quiet streets and courts, where taking short cuts I lose my way oft-times, spring up old familiar faces to remind me of the months spent on Spring Hill. The sentries at Whitehall relax from the discharge of their important duty of guarding nothing to give me a smile of recognition; the very newspaper offices look friendly as I pass them by; busy Printing-house Yard puts on a cheering smile, and the *Punch* office in Fleet Street sometimes laughs outright. Now, would all this have happened if I had returned to England a rich woman? Surely not.

A few words more ere I bring these egotistical remarks to a close. It is naturally with feelings of pride and pleasure that I allude to the committee recently organized to aid me; and if I indulge in the vanity of placing their names before my readers, it is simply because every one of the following noblemen and gentlemen knew me in the Crimea, and by consenting to assist me now record publicly their opinion of my services there. And yet I may reasonably on other grounds be proud of the fact, that it has been stated publicly that my present embarrassments originated in my charities and incessant labours among the army, by

> Major-General Lord Rokeby, K.C.B.
> H.S.H. Prince Edward of Saxe Weimar, C.B.
> His Grace the Duke of Wellington.
> His Grace the Duke of Newcastle.
> The Right Hon. Lord Ward.
> General Sir John Burgoyne, K.C.B.
> Major-General Sir Richard Airey, K.C.B.
> Rear-Admiral Sir Stephen Lushington, K.C.B.
> Colonel M'Murdo, C.B.
> Colonel Chapman, C.B.
> Lieutenant-Colonel Ridley, C.B.
> Major the Hon. F. Keane.
> W. H. Russell, Esq. (*Times* Correspondent).
> W. T. Doyne, Esq.

THE END.

London: Printed by Thomas Harrild, 11, Salisbury Square, Fleet Street.